# SECRET SPORTS PSYCHOLOGY REVEALED

## PROVEN TECHNIQUES TO ELEVATE YOUR PERFORMANCE

## RICK WOLFF

Skyhorse Publishing

Copyright © 2018 by Pond Lane Productions, Inc.

All rights reserved. No part of this book may be reproduced in any manner without the express written consent of the publisher, except in the case of brief excerpts in critical reviews or articles. All inquiries should be addressed to Skyhorse Publishing, 307 West 36th Street, 11th Floor, New York, NY 10018.

Skyhorse Publishing books may be purchased in bulk at special discounts for sales promotion, corporate gifts, fund-raising, or educational purposes. Special editions can also be created to specifications. For details, contact the Special Sales Department, Skyhorse Publishing, 307 West 36th Street, 11th Floor, New York, NY 10018 or info@skyhorsepublishing.com.

Skyhorse® and Skyhorse Publishing® are registered trademarks of Skyhorse Publishing, Inc.®, a Delaware corporation.

Visit our website at www.skyhorsepublishing.com.

10 9 8 7 6 5 4 3 2 1

Library of Congress Cataloging-in-Publication Data is available on file.

Cover design by Tom Lau
Cover illustration: iStockphoto

Print ISBN: 978-1-5107-1637-7
Ebook ISBN: 978-1-5107-1638-4

Printed in the United States of America

"So what are you going to do about it?"

—Harvey Dorfman, when confronting a struggling athlete

# ADVANCE PRAISE FOR
## *SECRETS OF SPORTS PSYCHOLOGY REVEALED*:

"There's a substantial amount of confusion and mystery surrounding sports psychology. But if you want a highly readable primer that cuts through all the clutter, I'd highly recommend Rick Wolff's *Secrets of Sports Psychology Revealed*. It contains tremendous insights for any top athlete."

—JOHN HART, former General Manager for theCleveland Indians, Texas Rangers, and Atlanta Braves

"I met Rick as a young minor-league player, close to thirty years ago. He was my introduction to sports psychology, making a big impact during the most formative years of my professional career. Rick helped me better understand how to handle the successes and inevitable failures associated with high competition. To this day I consider his counseling to have been an important element in my maturation as a baseball person, and even in my ongoing efforts to be prepared for what comes next."

—JERRY DIPOTO, Executive Vice President and General Manager, Seattle Mariners

"Every winner in athletics, business, medicine, etc. demonstrates qualities that you can observe as well as those inner attributes that you can't visually see. Rick Wolff, in his latest book, clearly defines and illustrates, in a practical way, how you can improve your performance both on the field as well as from behind your desk. His proven approach will be a guide for you to personally enhance your mental and emotional skills."

—AL GOLDIS, former major-league executive and member of the Baseball Scouts Hall of Fame

"Through his unique first-hand experience, Rick Wolff is able to consider the evolution of sports psychology and provide each athlete with easily applied tools and approaches to elevate his or her game. The mental side of sport is the key to bridging the gap between potential and performance and Rick's *Secrets of Sports Psychology Revealed* will provide anyone interested in elevating their game with easily applied approaches to consistent, improved mental performance."

—MARK A. SHAPIRO, President and CEO, Toronto Blue Jays

"We in baseball face a daunting task of trying to discern which player has that little 'extra' that will propel him to the major-league level ahead of others of the same skill sets. There are many aspiring athletes out there who want nothing more than to ascend to that next stratum. Rick Wolff in his new book can help you achieve that goal with his use of mental cue cards, muscle memory and visualization techniques to augment your physical skills. He breaks down problem areas—believing in oneself, dealing with nervousness, and working through adversity and turns them into positives. Any coach or aspiring player needs to read this book to learn the secrets of being ahead of the competition before the game even begins. If you're interested in elevating your game and leaving behind some of those stumbling blocks of the past, then this book can only expedite the accomplishment of your goals. Physical ability takes you so far, but the mental and psychological sides of your persona shape your destiny. Read it and you'll be ahead of the competition."

—JOE McILVAINE, Senior Advisor, Baltimore Orioles

"The difference between success and failure between the lines is in your head—remember, most hitters enshrined in Cooperstown failed in 7 of every 10 at-bats in their Hall-of-Fame careers. Rick ventured early into the world of sports psychology, and his approach to performance has helped athletes in all sports achieve from the little to the big leagues. This is a valuable read for athletes and coaches alike."

—GEORGE C. PAPPAS, International and Minor League Operations, Tampa Bay Rays, and author of *A Tribe Reborn: How the Cleveland Indians of the '90s Went from Cellar Dwellers to Playoff Contenders*

# CONTENTS

# A LITTLE BACKGROUND...

I FIRST BECAME OBSESSED WITH sports psychology in the early 1970s when I was an undergraduate at Harvard. Although not very well known, Harvard's baseball team during that time was more than just good—it was one of the top baseball college programs in the nation. Not only did the Crimson win the Ivy League crown seemingly year after year, but in my sophomore year (1971) we advanced all the way to the Division I College World Series in Omaha.

Harvard returned to the College World Series again in 1973 and 1974, but by then I had already been drafted and signed by the Detroit Tigers. And just for the record, the Crimson played in the CWS in 1968 as well, so appearing in the Elite Eight in Omaha on a fairly regular basis was no fluke.

From the team I played on, we had something like eight or nine players drafted into pro ball. Pete Varney, our All–Ivy League slugging catcher, was a first-round draft choice by the Chicago White

Sox and played several years in the big leagues (Ivy League football fans will recall that Pete also caught the "winning" two-point conversion against Yale in the famous 29–29 tie game). In any event, as a 6-foot, 165-lb. second baseman, I had excellent speed, range, and sprayed the ball to all fields. But like any aspiring ballplayer, I always fell prone to the occasional batting slump. To counter this, I spent countless hours in the batting cage, trying to hone and finesse my skills to such a fine point that I would, ideally, never again get fooled by a curveball or foul off a fastball that was right down the middle.

In my view, I should be able to "train" my muscles to react instantaneously, and in just the right way, no matter what the pitch. In my perspective, if I could master this basic psychological approach, I should be able to hit, and hit well, at any level of pro ball.

But as I searched the psychology text books in Harvard's esteemed and plentiful libraries (this was long before the Internet and Google had been invented), one reality become very clear to me: there were no practical books on sports psychology. This was an entirely brand new field which had been left unexplored.

It was right around this time that the East German Olympic athletes were experimenting with applied sports psychology, but what little data I could find was abstract, and in fact, hard to apply. Looking back, I also realize that the East Germans were not eager to share their psychological insights with the rest of the world.

But as someone who was determined to find and develop any kind of mental advantage to my game, I dove in and read as many related books I could find on such "new" terms as muscle memory, visualization, mental cue cards, and so on. Remember, these concepts were not well known back then. And of course, there were no sports psychologists working with pro or college athletes. It was a discipline that just didn't exist.

There was also a very conservative attitude in pro sports during those days. Big-league front offices and coaches frowned on new developments. Indeed, by the time I was playing professional baseball in the mid-1970s, the generally accepted outlook on sports psychology went like this: *Any player who needs to see a sports psychologist ought to have his head examined.*

Yes, it's a funny line, but that was the perception.

Left to my own devices, I started to search for psychology books whose insights could be adapted to sports. One of the very first I read was a book on something called visualization by a successful surgeon, Dr. Maxwell Maltz. His book, *Psycho-Cybernetics*, which was originally published in 1960, and is still in print today and continues to sell, detailed how he prepared for an operation. In short, he would try to "train" his hand and finger muscles by "visualizing" each precise step of the procedure. He would "see" and plan in his head every aspect of the operation, from beginning to end, and only then did he feel fully prepared to go ahead with performing the actual surgery.

In effect, this was his way of explaining visualization and muscle memory. And it made sense to me. I started to adapt Dr. Maltz's approach to the way I mentally prepared for every game I played in.

Did it always work? Well, let's put it this way. By following this visualization approach, I always entered a game knowing that I was mentally ready, fully focused, and ready to perform at the best of my athletic abilities. Did this ensure that I always hit the ball solidly every at-bat, or that I made every play in the field? No, of course not; nobody can guarantee that. But I did play each and every game with a sense of mental preparedness that raised my game to a higher level.

And in short, that's really the goal of sports psychology: *to raise your sense of readiness so that you can compete at the peak of your athletic potential.*

## MY OWN LUCKY BREAK

Some years after my playing career and while I was coaching at the collegiate level, I wrote a book based on what little research I could find on sports psychology. *The Psychology of Winning Baseball* was published by Prentice-Hall in 1986, and the publication of that book led to an exciting and unforeseen development in my life.

In 1989, I received a call from Harvey Dorfman, who was the roving sports psychology coach for the Oakland A's. Harvey was Oakland's "secret weapon" in that he counseled and guided ballplayers and coaches on how to confront their fears and anxieties so they could play their game at a higher level. As you might recall, the Oakland Athletics were the dominant team in major-league baseball in the late 1980s.

Dorfman told me that he had read my book and knew that I had played pro ball and had been a successful head college coach. He said that a number of major-league teams had contacted him about his jumping over to their team. But Harvey was content working for Oakland, so he asked me if he could give the other teams my phone number. Flattered and stunned, I of course said yes.

Within a matter of a week, I heard from a half-dozen major-league general managers, all of whom had been sent my way by Harvey. I ultimately decided to sign with the then-lowly Cleveland Indians, mainly because their front office people at that time—Hank Peters, John Hart, and Dan O'Dowd—impressed me very much with their candid assessment of their organization, and their long-range plans to improve the team.

My role was to work with their current major leaguers, minor leaguers, and coaching staffs to help them gain a better understanding of basic sports psychology principles and how to apply those principles to their respective abilities.

But along the way, I explained to the front office: "If you expect me to tell your players just to think positive thoughts all the time ... or to just take deep breaths when they're anxious in a game ... or to just listen to inspirational music in order to improve their skills, then you've hired the wrong guy.

"In short, that kind of stuff really doesn't work. It's just superficial and artificial."

Within five years, the Indians—long the laughing stock of major-league baseball (remember the hit movie *Major League*?) routinely playing in front of less than 5,000 fans in cavernous old Memorial Stadium in Cleveland—went on to win the American League pennant in 1995.

Was I responsible for that turnaround? Of course not. As noted, the Tribe had a terrific and very smart front office, talented scouts, and most importantly, they had outstanding ballplayers. But I do take pride in that I worked with a number of their players in my years with the organization and that perhaps I had a little impact in their approach to their game.

## WHAT THIS BOOK WILL COVER

"Just take some deep breaths and calm yourself down..."

How many times have you heard that kind of advice from your coach when you were in a tight spot in a game?

I don't know about you, but as a former professional ballplayer, while I agree that you certainly need to breathe during the game, just taking a deep breath or two in order to relax never really did much for me when I was competing. The same goes for just thinking positive thoughts. Perhaps, of course, that kind of simplistic advice works for some athletes, but in my years of clinical work, I never found that those solutions offered much.

That's why I decided to write this book. As the world of sports psychology has grown exponentially over the last thirty years, I felt that the time had come to write an easy-to-read, and hopefully easy-to-implement, field guide for those athletes who want to include a solid and practical mental approach to improve their game.

If you consider yourself to be a topflight athlete, or you aspire to be one, trust me: you will need a systematic and organized approach with your mental game. And to that end, what I have attempted to do in this book is to present you with a series of easy-to-follow steps and guidelines to get you on the right track.

Will all of my insights work for you? No. But hopefully, what my bits of advice will make you do is think about how you go about preparing for each contest, and more importantly, how you can spontaneously make mental adjustments during the game when the situation calls for it.

Let's face it. For most of you, when you were a kid, chances are you were so gifted physically that you just went out to play and dominated mainly because you were just so much better than all the other kids. You probably didn't give much thought at all to your mental game. Perhaps you listened to some sweet music on your iPod as a way to clear your mind or to psych yourself up for the game. That's fine, and you should continue to do that. But beyond that, I would wager that when you were in high school you probably didn't need to do much in terms of psychologically preparing yourself for your next game.

But as you climbed the ladder of competition, either to the next level in college or to an elite travel team or perhaps to a professional level, you started to look around and you noticed a few important changes. For starters, now everybody is much bigger, faster, and better than your high school teammates. And the game itself is played at a higher—and better—level. If you want to compete against them, you're going to have to step up your game. And to help you do just that, beginning to focus on the psychological element is an important first step in your development.

To that end, this book will be different. I want to provide eager and serious athletes some real prescriptive guidelines as to what they can do *right now* to improve their mental game. My advice is based upon real-world practices, taken from the work I've done with top athletes over the years.

To me, the key has always been trying to first help the athlete confront the immediate issue or problem at hand. Get the athlete to come to grips with it, and then tailor and develop a responsible and conscientious process to eliminate the problem that holds the athlete back. And as noted, it's important to give the athlete some mental cues on how to make vital adjustments during the heat of their game.

Most importantly, you need to keep in mind that sports psychology is not a cure-all. It is not designed to perform miracles. Yet when administered properly, it can offer you the potential of superb results. Best of all, just as you have control over your physical game in terms of your conditioning and practice, you will come away with a much stronger mental approach of how to prepare for each game.

## PREPARE YOUR MIND IN THE SAME WAY YOU PREPARE YOUR BODY

You give serious thought to your pregame meal, correct? Or how you practice each day, right?

Those are essential steps that are key to one's physical well-being.

But remarkably too few athletes spend much time thinking about how they're going to prepare their mind for the next game. Knowing how to think about, and mentally prepare for, a game is a major component of sports psychology. And yet, most athletes—including many of the best—never really give the mental approach much thought.

Why is that?

Well, the answer is pretty simple. Because, as noted, so many top athletes have done so well for so long in their sport that they have never really had to give any thought to their pregame mental preparation. After all, if you were born with unique special skills, e.g., superior size, speed, eye-hand coordination, strength, and so on, then you just pretty much walked out onto the field and immediately dominated. And have always done so.

As such, there probably wasn't much of a need to "think" about your next game—except to make sure you got plenty of sleep the night before, and had a decent pregame meal. And of course, to pay attention to what the coach had in mind in terms of game strategy.

But here's the reality. As all athletes continue to ascend the pyr-amid of competition, they discover that going from one level to the next becomes more difficult. It was easy for them to dominate at the youth level, and even in high school or on local travel teams. But once they arrive at the collegiate level, suddenly, for the first time in their life, they are now confronted with other superior athletes who are probably just as big, fast, strong, and talented as they are.

Presented with this new kind of level playing field, it's now up to the athlete to figure out some sort of new advantage around their competitors. And for many, exploring the world of sports psychol-ogy and trying to find a fresh approach on how to prepare them-selves mentally becomes critically important.

That's one of the key purposes of this book.

So, ask yourself: what do you do to mentally prepare for a game?

If you don't do much, or have never thought about what you do, that's to be expected. And that's fine.

But my goal is to not only make you aware that this mental approach exists, but that following some of the tips I present here will help you elevate your game, and ideally make you more consis-tent in your performances. Besides, there's a good chance that your opponents are already exploring sports psychology as well.

But by the end of this book, it is hoped that you will:

- Have a basic understanding of sports psychology
- Discover some of the myths and misconceptions of the topic
- Learn how to better prepare yourself mentally for games
- Be able to customize and streamline your ability to make key adjustments during the heat of competition
- Learn how to cope with setbacks, and more importantly, what steps can be taken to learn from your mistakes and defeats

Does all of this take a little time? Yes. But you'll find that once you start, you'll discover quickly that your approach will become more focused on what you want to achieve, and how you can do so.

You will also find that I have attempted to write this book in a breezy style. Over the years, I have found that too many sports psychology guides, manuals, and books tend to read in a kind of academic, dry, mumbo-jumbo nomenclature that really isn't accessible to many readers. True, some of these books often contain wonderful psychological research and have great insights, but I have always been bothered by their seemingly high-brow vocabulary that unfortunately makes their work difficult to follow and to implement.

Having been a college and pro player myself, as well as a college head coach and professional coach, I know that athletes are always eager for new insights and information. But they also want that kind of intel presented to them in a manner that is easy to understand and easy to apply right away.

For that reason, I've attempted to write this book in that kind of style; that is, a casual approach that tries to connect the latest thoughts and research on sports psychology with the insights from the various top athletes I've had the privilege of working with over the years.

So let's get started.

Rick Wolff
Fall 2017

# 1

# AN INTRODUCTION TO SPORTS PSYCHOLOGY

"It was a really tough thirty minutes for me that hopefully I never experience again."

Those were the words of Jordan Spieth right after the 2016 Masters golf tournament when, after cruising along seemingly effortlessly for three days with a five-shot lead heading to the 10th tee on the final back nine, Spieth uncharacteristically fell apart with consecutive bogeys followed by a quadruple bogey before putting the brakes on this unexpected meltdown.

Problem was, by the time the twenty-two-year-old Spieth had recovered his bearings, his 5-shot lead had evaporated and Danny Willett, a not-well-known Englishman, had taken over the lead and never looked back. Willett won the tournament, a tournament he didn't expect to play in. He had actually circled the date on his calendar, but because his wife was due with their first child at the same time, Willet assumed he would be at her side instead of competing.

But their son arrived a bit earlier than expected, and as such, Willett headed to Georgia to compete.

By the way, although the sports world focused its attention on the travails of Spieth, what was overlooked was that Willett was five shots behind Spieth with just six holes to play. While Jordan was collapsing, Danny shot a 5-under 67 for the day, which matched the best score of the weekend. He had no bogeys in his last round.

Put another way, while Spieth was having fits down the stretch, Willett was calmly going about his business. I'm quite sure he was well aware of what has happening to Spieth's lead, but Willett found a way to play his game and not be distracted.

I use this example from the world of golf because in many ways, it symbolizes what kind of role sports psychology can play in highly competitive events. While there might have been some technical adjustments that Jordan should have made to his game when he was going through this rough patch, the truth is that, physically, he was in good shape. He wasn't tired, or weak, or in poor health. He just made some bad decisions on his shots, and as he tried to salvage his game, he apparently made some more poor decisions.

This takes us into the realm of sports psychology.

On the other hand, Danny didn't allow the building excitement or adrenaline rush get in the way of his game. He played on with a stoic approach, not allowing the unexpected developments to impede or get in the way of his mental approach.

One fateful afternoon of golf. Two amazingly talented golfers. And yet, one was able to maintain a solid mental focus while the other apparently fell victim to psychological disaster.

That evening and for the next few days, sports radio talk shows were filled with callers who had compassionate advice for Jordan Spieth:

"What he needs to do is to go out right away on Augusta National and play those three holes he screwed up on, and play them again. He needs to convince himself that he can handle and master those holes. Otherwise, he'll be plagued forever by that memory of disaster."

Someone else said just the opposite: "C'mon, the guy's a top pro. Best thing for him to do is just shake it off and forget about it. Go out and have a couple of beers and don't give it a second thought. Hey, it's golf—that kind of thing happens."

So, if you were to meet up with Jordan Spieth, and after you expressed your sympathies for his tough performance at the Masters, what kind of advice would you give him to bounce back?

Or, what would you advise a baseball player who is stuck in a horrendous batting slump?

Or a basketball player who can't seem to sink free throws with any real consistency, especially at the end of a game when the score is close?

Or a field goal kicker who has a very strong and accurate leg, but also seems to have difficulty in delivering in clutch situations?

*If there is one target goal you want to learn about and take away from this book, it's the concept of how to get "into the zone" . . . That's the ultimate reward.*

## BUT FIRST, A LITTLE HOMEWORK

There are all sorts of ways to get into the psychology of improving your performance. But let's start with the basic presumption that, in an ideal world, top athletes are always hoping to be able to slow the action down in the heat of competition and to focus on what they can do and how they can do it.

In short, to perform at a high level on a consistent basis.

Sure, physical talent and repetitive practice are essential. But once you begin to climb the steep slope of the athletic pyramid, you begin to recognize that all of your competitors are pretty much just like you: they are physically talented and, like you, they have devoted most of their life to endless practice to improve and hone their skills.

Don't believe me? Be sure to Google the 2017 Gatorade commercial about difference makers featuring current NFL superstar J. J. Watt. That short, entertaining, and powerful commercial does a terrific job in highlighting how you and all of your competitors are all working your tails off in order to get a competitive advantage.

So, if your peers are top athletes—just like you—how does one reach the next level where they not only compete . . . but also win?

Think about that.

Let me explain so there's no misunderstanding. Let's say you're hoping to someday play on a college team. Or you have your sights set on someday playing at the professional level. If that's true, then you owe it to yourself to take a few minutes to do a little homework on the athletic accomplishments of some of today's college and pro stars.

To do that, choose a few of your favorite athletes. Go online and Google them. Go to their Wikipedia page, or if you want, go to the college website where they currently play, or to the website for their pro team.

Scan quickly down to their high school achievements. You'll see that no matter where that individual grew up—whether it was in Orlando or Topeka or Spokane or wherever—that athlete won all sorts of accolades and awards in their youth. All-League. All-County. All-State. Team captain. League MVP. And so on.

And in many cases, these achievements weren't just in one sport, but a variety of sports, meaning that these athletes were so gifted that they didn't have to specialize in just one activity as a youth. In other words, these individuals were clearly viewed as top athletes when they were growing up.

Now, do this: take a few moments to check out some of the backgrounds of some of this athlete's teammates. Especially at the professional and Division I level, a quick scan of most of the other players on that team will reveal similar outstanding athletic accomplishments and achievements from when they were in high school. In short, there are a lot of top athletes in this country, they come from all over, and they all have terrific athletic resumes. And it should also be apparent that these individuals are totally dedicated to their sport, and stay in top shape all year round in order to remain at the top of their game.

My point is this: *If there are so many top, top athletes out there, and all of them are accomplished, and all of them are eager to compete and win, what becomes the critically important element in their drive to succeed as they take the field, court, or ice?*

When I was working with the Cleveland Indians, I recall discussing this very point with a number of the major leaguers as well as with other top professional athletes. And they all pointed to one element: *the mental side of their game.* They just felt that in addition to all of their physical preparation, such as running, lifting, skill training, and practice, as they climbed up higher on the pyramid of athletic competition, they found that they could no longer just depend on their God-given athletic skills. Instead, they needed to spend an ample amount of time working on their individual mental approach to each game.

That is, as a youngster or as a high school athlete, they worked hard on developing their physical game, and for the most part, they were so good at running, jumping, catching, throwing, hitting, and so on that so long as they felt physically ready to go when the games began, they would not only succeed, but would often dominate.

But that situation changes dramatically when such athletes reach the next level in sports. Invariably, that quantum leap from, say, high school or travel team to college is often a leap that very few athletes are prepared for. For the first time in their athletic careers, they are confronted with facing other top competitors who are just as talented, as big, and as fast as they are. Suddenly, it's as though they have become . . . *average.*

No longer a big fish in a small pond—but now an average fish in a much bigger pond—deep down these athletes start to worry about how they are going to find a way to prove that they are superior to all of their new teammates. In some cases, they just don't match up. A player who was a star 6-foot-4 center on his high school basketball team suddenly discovers on his college team that there are 6-foot-4 guards and that the centers and forwards he's competing against are 6-foot-8 or taller, and they are just as coordinated as he is. In those kinds of cases, the player has some important decisions to make: Do I quit? Do I understand that I won't get much playing time? Or do I consider transferring to a less competitive basketball program?

The point is, physically, he's just not going to be able to match up. And from a psychological perspective, this is also quite a blow to a youngster who has been a star. In short, it's a very hard transition.

Now, what about the kid who is 6-foot-8 and who does have the physical skills and talent to compete against that level of competition? What does he have to do in order to impress the coaching staff in order to make the starting five?

In other words, when you have two or more top athletes competing against each other and they all have similar physical skills, what makes the difference between one of them being more consistent and more productive in their play than another? From a coach's point of view, invariably, that's what you want: a player who delivers on a consistent basis, someone you can count on during the tough games.

This is when lots of athletes begin to search for that extra edge—and that's where the mental side becomes a part of their everyday life. Athletes want to know how to shut out any and all distractions so they can perform at a higher level. They want to be focused on the task at hand that they are not even aware of the crowd cheering, even though the stadium is packed and is rocking. They just wanted the game to slow down so that they could play at a consistently high level.

In other words, they wanted to be "in the zone." Why? Because when you reach it, your entire body and brain are totally synced and locked in—and all of your hard work at practice, combined with your God-given talent, come together with just the right mental balance to allow you to perform at your peak ability.

That's the ultimate aim of sports psychology.

And that's the purpose of this book. To try and elevate you to the highest level of your athletic ability.

Is this easy? No. Are there are any guarantees? No. Do you have to be able to understand a lot of psychobabble mumble-jumble? No.

But one thing is for sure. If you don't have a grasp of what the mental game is about, you're going to be heading into direct competition with other top athletes who do. And that puts you in a very distinct disadvantage.

## "LOOK AT YOURSELF IN THE MIRROR . . . AND DO IT NOW!"

Let me take a moment to tell you about Harvey Dorfman, who did more to revolutionize the field of sports psychology than anybody else over the last forty years.

Harvey, who passed away at age seventy-five a few years ago, was a former high school English teacher who grew up in the Bronx before eventually marrying and then moving his wife and kids to rural Vermont where he taught at a local private school. Plagued his entire life with a shortness of breath that caused him to cough every few seconds, Harvey loved all sports, was super competitive, and despite his breathing disability, was good enough to become a goalkeeper for his college soccer team.

A prolific reader of serious literature and a superb writer as well, Harvey—he penned his books as H. A. Dorfman—used to spend his summers watching the Class AA farm team of the old Montreal Expos in Vermont. Bit by bit, he befriended Karl Kuehl, who was the farm director for the Expos and before long, Dorfman was providing helpful mental insights to some of the players.

This was all taking place in the early 1980s when, as I mentioned above, the world of sports psychology was not really well accepted in pro sports. Dorfman was truly a pioneer in the world of baseball, especially when Kuehl (who had moved onto the Oakland Athletics) hired him to work as their roving sports psychology coach.

Let me put this into perspective. This move was unheard of. Absolutely revolutionary stuff. No other professional baseball organization at that time—in fact, I'll bet that no pro team of any kind—had a mental skills coach on their payroll.

Also, bear in mind that Harvey was trained as an English teacher. He didn't have a doctorate in psychology. And except for coaching the girls' varsity basketball team for a year or two, he really hadn't coached at any level. In other words, he was an educator with no background in psychology or even baseball for that matter.

But Harvey had a distinctive talent when it came to communicating with athletes. He was blessed with a gravelly voice that boomed no matter where he was. To make ballplayers feel more comfortable in talking with him, Dorfman deliberately sprinkled his language with all sorts of profanities. And he sure wasn't bashful. He didn't care who you were, or how big a star you were ... he knew how to get into your face, and as he said, would force you to "look in the mirror at yourself."

This was Harvey's blunt approach—direct and confrontational. I remember him telling me over and over again, "Rick, if you want to simply tell these major-league baseball players to just think pure and positive thoughts, or to allow them to make excuses for themselves, well, you're wasting your time—and theirs as well."

Dorfman would say, "My job is to do what their posse or entourage is not doing. These hangers-on are surrounding the athlete, telling him how great he is, and how talented he is ... when what the ballplayer really needs to hear is that he's not getting the job done."

Dorfman would be fired up by now: "Even today's managers and coaches won't tell these guys the truth ... they're afraid that they will insult them and as a result, will lose any thread of a relationship with their star player.

"But that's what these guys need ... somebody to make them accountable. Somebody to hold up a mirror to their face and say, 'Look, you're hitting less than .200, or you're not throwing strikes and your ERA is sky-high.'

"And then I tell them, flat out: 'What are you going to about your lousy performance? Don't look to me for the answers, because I don't have any. It's all up to you to figure out the answer. Do you need to go back and watch more videotape and pay close attention? Do you need to start making more adjustments during the game? Do you need to get back into physical shape? Whatever the solution is, it's in you ... and you're getting paid a lot of money to find the answer!'"

When I first saw Harvey do this with a promising young major leaguer, I was stunned. It was so in-your-face, I didn't know what would happen. And yet, the young star listened intently and when Harvey stopped to catch his breath and cough, the kid jumped up and profusely thanked him: "Harvey, nobody has ever had the guts to tell me the truth about myself. I've always had someone around me to make an excuse for me whenever I fell into a slump. But the truth is ... I *hear* you. I need to step up for myself, once and for all, and start pinpointing what I need to do to get back on the right track."

As noted, I was stunned watching this.

But I saw Harvey do this countless times with not just rising minor leaguers, but also with established major-league All-Stars. He had the courage to tell them what they didn't want to hear—that not only were they not performing well, but that the fault was *theirs*.

Dorfman didn't want to hear about alibis or excuses. He wouldn't allow it. If you offered an excuse for a poor effort or performance, he would simply say, "Oh, OK ... if that's the best you can do, well, then that's it. Good luck with your next life after sports, because you're clearly close to the end. But I, for one, don't believe you have topped out in sports. And I don't think you believe it either."

It's not that Harvey shamed the player. Rather, he motivated him psychologically to want to rise to the challenge.

Now, I'm of course paraphrasing Harvey's approach and unique style. And he worked with players on a long-term basis; I don't want to give one the impression that he simply delivered a fiery pep talk to an athlete and the job was complete. Harvey knew that players are always looking for psychological guidance and support, and need someone like Harvey to let them know when they were starting to go off the rails.

During his long career of working with top athletes, Harvey would never discuss who his clients were with the general media or with anyone else, for that matter. But one day, when I was visiting him at his home in North Carolina, I had a chance to walk around his office. On the walls were photos of big-league stars, several of whom would go onto the Hall of Fame. The photos were personally inscribed, "Harvey, how can I ever repay you for all of your help?" or, "If it weren't for you, Harv, I would have never lasted in this game."

The personal testaments to Dorfman's communication skills were amazing, and there were dozens of them. In recent years some of these star athletes have come forward to pay tribute to his psychological magic. One of the most outspoken—and grateful—is former major-league pitcher Jamie Moyer, the oldest pitcher ever to win a game in the big leagues (he did it when he was forty-nine). And as Jamie makes clear in his recent autobiography, *Just Tell Me I Can't*, if it weren't for a chance conversation with Dorfman, Moyer was on his way out of baseball.

Jamie Moyer was a soft-tossing left-hander who had enjoyed some success in the minors. But at the big-league level, he felt compelled that he had to somehow learn to throw harder in order to succeed. He feared that if he tried to throw inside to major-league hitters, he would be hit hard. As a result, Moyer avoided it, and this eventually caught up with him.

But Dorfman talked with him, and began to challenge him to trust himself when he changed speeds on the mound, and before too long Moyer began to see significant results. His career seemed to last forever. For the next twenty years, Moyer was that rare big-league pitcher who lived by changing speeds and not throwing 90 mph fastballs. Moyer credits all of his success to Dorfman, who liberated the courage in Moyer to do what he does best on the mound.

Harvey was a singular force of nature, a rare human being. His home was filled with wall after wall of bookshelves. He was just as comfortable reading the *New York Times Book Review* each Sunday as he was going through a box score from the sports pages. Most importantly, he knew how to connect with athletes. How to cut through the veneer of insecurity. How to get them to tell him the truth about what was really bothering them.

As an athlete, this is really the first step in opening your mind to sports psychology. You have to learn how to be objective and honest with yourself. Put all of your newspaper clippings, headlines, and video highlight reels away. If you want to get better in your sport, it's time to learn how to be honest about what you do well, and what you need to improve upon.

As you might recall from earlier in the book, it was Harvey Dorfman who recommended me to a number of big-league general managers. Ultimately, I signed with the Cleveland Indians because their front office was eager to take the next step in terms of sports psychology for their athletes, and I was impressed with their commitment to the task at hand.

I started to make the rounds in spring training in 1990 with the Indians, getting to know the players and the coaches in a friendly manner. I wanted them to see me as someone who could help—not as someone who represented a threat from the front office.

Once again, Dorfman played a key role by giving me some valuable advice as to how to accelerate my acceptance by the players. "Rick, these guys are instinctively going to be very, very sensitive to talking with any kind of shrink who shows up in a suit and tie," he told me. "So do what I do. Get into a uniform and show the guys that you are comfortable around the game. If you can, hit some fungoes to the infielders in spring training. Throw some batting practice. The more they see that you were a real player, the quicker they will accept you and talk with you."

It was excellent advice. And Harvey was absolutely correct. Remember, this is in spring training, 1990. Sports psychologists were still very rare, and most ballplayers were, at best, somewhat suspicious of being seen talking to a sports shrink. But once the Indians saw me not only in uniform on the field, but also shagging flies, throwing BP, and hitting fungoes, they began to sense I could relate to the game as a player. And when the word got around that I had been drafted and played in the Detroit Tigers' organization, they all began to relax and lighten up around me. In short, whatever resistant psychological barriers had existed were now gone.

Making that connection and building that sense of trust with the ballplayers is, of course, crucial to connecting with them. As noted, Dorfman was always in uniform around the players he counseled, and even though as he didn't throw batting practice, Harvey's demeanor, loud voice, and easiness around the players made them all feel as though he belonged. He was truly one of them. And I made every attempt to do the same.

Fast forward to now. These days, several major-league baseball teams have sports psychology coaches on their staff, which is great. But the truth is, only a small number of these coaches dress out in uniform to talk with the players. Perhaps that's because, with the passage of time, sports psychologists have become better accepted by today's athletes. But back when I started with Cleveland, as per Harvey Dorfman's strong suggestion, I found that wearing the uniform was a big help.

## A QUICK BUT ENJOYABLE DETOUR

In 1989, I was assigned by *Sports Illustrated* to write a piece about how difficult it is to play in the low minor leagues. This was around the time that the classic movie *Field of Dreams* was in the theatres and was portraying baseball in a wonderful and positive feel-good light. In any event, the only stipulation from *Sports Illustrated* was that I had to be signed by a pro team and get into two or three games as an active player.

At this point in my life, I was thirty-eight years old, and I hadn't played professionally since I was twenty-four. And as I pointed out to the editor at *Sports Illustrated*, it was hard enough getting signed when I was twenty-one—it was only going to be that much tougher at age thirty-eight.

Nevertheless, that was the assignment. But I caught a break. Al Goldis, who had coached me in the college summer leagues, was now serving as the director of scouting for the Chicago White Sox. Al told me that the South Bend White Sox had just clinched the first half of the Midwest League, and had a few games in hand before the start of the second half of the season. If I signed all the insurance papers stating that if I got myself killed playing for South Bend I wouldn't sue anyone, he'd send me a contract.

He did, and I played three games in South Bend.

Long story short, I went 4-for-7 (a .571 batting average) with three RBIs including a double off the center-field fence. Not bad for an old guy playing against top athletes in their early twenties, and facing pitchers throwing 90 mph fastballs.

## "HOW THE HELL ARE YOU DOING THIS?"

Perhaps the greatest compliment came from the nineteen-year-old who was playing shortstop for South Bend (I was playing second base). After I smacked another line-drive hit, he asked me, "No offense, mister, but how the hell are you doing this?"

It was a funny question, but deep down, I think he was serious. And the more I thought about it, I do think that psychology was at the base of my success. I really went into this short venture in Class A ball with no expectations. Remember, the column I was going to write for *SI* was supposed to be about how tough it is to survive in pro ball.

As a result, I wasn't really tense or anxious or nervous during my at-bats. After all, there was no pressure on me to get a hit. Everybody just assumed I'd look at three strikes and go back to the dugout and sit down. But being an athlete, I also didn't want to embarrass myself. All I focused on was just seeing the pitch to the plate, and nothing more. I needed to trust my athletic skills, even though I hadn't played in a long time.

Sounds like basic common sense. But when you're competing for real, whether you acknowledge it or not, you are bringing an entire agenda—a real psychological burden—to each performance, e.g., I want to do well, I need to do well, I need to get a hit, I want to impress the coaching staff, the scouts, my family, and so on. These unspoken pressures accompany you when you take the field or the court or the ice. And trust me, these underlying pressures can take their toll on you if you let them.

Clear your head. Clear your mind. Don't encumber your mind with those pressures that can get in the way of your athletic ability. Don't sabotage yourself with extra pressure.

Let me give you an example. I recall asking Jim Thome, the great power hitter who came up through the Indians' minor-league system, what went through his mind when he went to the plate. He thought about the question and then said to me, "All I concentrate on is seeing the pitch. That's all that I focus on. I clear my mind as I walk to the batter's box of everything else except ... see the pitch ... and react to it."

Straightforward, but powerful advice. You have to leave all the pregame psychological clutter back in the dugout or on the bench. You now just have to rely upon your instinct and athletic skill.

Yes, that's hard to do. But that's where you need to learn to trust your athletic skills and preparation. That's the key. I'll have more on how to do this in a later chapter.

Here's another example. A few months ago, I was listening to WFAN Sports Radio and Amani Toomer, the gifted wide receiver who played for several years in the NFL, was being asked why Eli Manning, the quarterback for the New York Giants, was able to play so well in the playoffs whereas his older brother, Peyton, always seemed to have difficulty in winning playoff games. Of course, both

Eli and Peyton both won two Super Bowls in their respective careers, but Eli (who was still active in 2017) is 8–4 in the playoff games he's started, whereas Peyton was only 14–13 in the playoffs.

Toomer acknowledged that both Manning brothers prepared diligently for postseason games, and of course, both had superb physical skills. But Toomer made an interesting observation about Eli. "To me, Eli just didn't seem to care," said Toomer. "Don't get me wrong. I'm sure he wanted to win, just like Peyton, but Eli went about his preparation and played in the games as through it really didn't matter to him whether he won or lost."

That was a curious and insightful observation. Toomer went onto explain that since Eli didn't seem to carry that extra psychological burden that he *had* to win or else, he was thus able to trust his athletic instincts more during the football games and to simply go with the flow. In other words, if Eli threw an interception, or was sacked on a play, he was able to simply walk away, and then come back, refreshed, and ready to try again the next time the Giants got the ball back. There was no sense of panic, or that he had to somehow force himself or push himself to play a higher level. He seemed to play with the inner sense that if he didn't put too much pressure on himself, then he could go on and play at his regular, almost relaxed pace, and that would allow him to play better.

The overall point regarding both Jim Thome and Eli Manning and countless other top pro athletes is that once the games begin, you *have* to allow yourself to play. Trust your instincts. If you have prepared properly, that's fine. But now is the time to allow all of your mental preparation to sit back, and to allow your physical skills and instincts to take over.

Can you still make adjustments throughout the game? Of course you can. And you should. But making adjustments in your approach *should not* get in the way of your trust in your physical skills. They need to all work together, not against each other. And don't allow your psychological concerns gum up the works!

It's my theory that when one's athletic skills are totally synced with one's psychological approach, that's the best pathway to reaching the zone—that rarified area where the game slows down for you and everything seems totally possible and accessible. We'll be discussing all of this in this book.

## A QUICK POSTSCRIPT TO MY SHORT STAY IN SOUTH BEND

Before I move on from that three-day stint in 1989 when I hit .571 for the South Bend White Sox, the story didn't end there. Some five years later, when I was working for the Indians as their roving sports psychology coach, I was at the old Municipal Stadium in Cleveland one evening before a game between the Indians and the visiting Chicago White Sox.

I was in uniform during batting practice, making the rounds with the Cleveland ballplayers. And my last name was on the back of my Indians' jersey. Now in my mid-forties, I was easy to spot as I was considerably older than the Indians' players.

Meanwhile, a number of White Sox pitchers had come out early to stretch and to get their running in. One of those pitchers was Scott Radinsky, a hard-throwing and talented left-hander. Scott, as luck would have it, had been one of my "teammates" on the South Bend team when I played there. When my stint in South Bend had come to an end, I had gone back to living the life of a middle-aged man with my wife and kids. But Scott had continued on his ascent in the minors and had advanced to the big leagues with Chicago.

But on that particular summer evening in Cleveland in the 1990s, he now spotted me in an Indians uniform and put it all together. Remember, he had seen me put on quite a show as a hitter some five years earlier. He came up to me, gave me a warm greeting, and asked, "So, Rick, are you now playing for the Indians? Did they sign you?"

He was indeed quite serious. He thought Cleveland had signed me to a contract as an ageless hitter.

And it was, without doubt, one of the finest compliments I have ever received in my sporting career.

# 2

# THE POSITIVE POWER OF SUPERSTITIONS

Do They Work? Yes . . . but only to a certain point.

One of the most commonly known psychological ploys is that of superstitions in sports.

For as long as most fans can remember, top athletes in every sport have come up and created all kinds of superstitions that, if followed precisely, should go a long way to helping ensure that the individual will maintain a high level of play.

There are, of course, countless superstitions. Most baseball fans recall that five-time batting champion Wade Boggs never ate anything but chicken for lunch on any day that he had a game. Older Boston Celtics basketball fans will chuckle at the memory that the team wouldn't be ready to go out to play until they heard their legendary center, Bill Russell, throw up in the bathroom before each game. Once Russell took care of his pregame nerves, his teammates could relax and could go out and play a focused game with confidence because of that unusual pregame superstition.

Of course, many athletes are so superstitious that they won't even talk about their innermost routines. But trust me, it's the rare athlete who doesn't have a peculiar or unique pregame habit that has become part of their mental preparation for an upcoming contest.

It doesn't take much to figure out that wearing a pair of lucky game socks, or driving along a special route to the ballpark, or listening to the same line-up of songs on one's iPod can be perceived as a simple cause and effect by the athlete. The reasoning is something like this:

*The last time I wore these particular socks, I had an amazing game. Thus, if I wear the same socks for my next game, then I should expect to have another great game.*

Or, at the very least, *I'm making a very conscious and concerted effort to help ensure the same results.*

And of course, if that one excellent game is followed by another game with a superior performance, then the athlete will definitely buy into the power of superstition. This is all the magic of cause and effect. In the athlete's mind, thanks to wearing special socks, they have ensured having another outstanding game.

Scientists everywhere will laugh out loud at this nonsensical conclusion. After all, how could following a simple superstition like that have any kind of positive impact upon one's performance in a competitive setting?

But then again, maybe it does. Consider the psychological impact of being reassured or comforted that you're going to perform well today because you're wearing your special socks. Doesn't that mental "security blanket" make you feel good? Wouldn't you want that kind of reassurance *before* you start the game? Not surprisingly, most top athletes do.

And if the superstition of your special socks doesn't work during tonight's game—and that of course often happens—then it's easy for the athlete to discard their "lucky" socks and start to look for another "magical" ritual or special piece of clothing that will help get them back on the right track.

But there's more to this. In one small but significant study conducted at the University of Cologne that was reported in the *Wall Street Journal* (April 29, 2010), a group of unsuspecting golfers on a putting green were told they were playing with a "lucky ball." As it developed, they sank 6.4 putts out of 10—which was nearly two more putts on average than a second group of golfers who weren't told their golf ball was lucky.

In other words, that suggestion of a "lucky ball" accounted for an improvement of 35 percent.

Coincidence? Or just superstition having a positive psychological impact?

"Our results suggest that the activation of a superstition can indeed yield performance improving effects," noted Lysann Damisch, who was the co-author of the Cologne study. To me, the overall conclusion—that believing in one's own good fortune can actually make one feel that "today is their day to shine"—cannot be discounted.

Confirms Stuart Vyse, a professor of psychology at Connecticut College, "Simply being told this is a lucky ball is sufficient to affect performance."

In that same *Wall Street Journal* article, outspoken Dallas Mavericks owner Mark Cuban, who is a big believer in statistics and analytics, is amazed by how much of a role superstition plays in his high-priced players: "Every locker room has a comical procession of superstitions." Continuing on, Cuban focused on the peculiar pregame activities of his players: "We have things based on time, on speech intonations, and on specific conversation exchanges. If you look at the introductions of any NBA team and what the players do, you have an anthropologist's dream."

So does this suggest that having a pregame superstition is OK? In my opinion, not only is it OK, but it's probably a welcome move. Assuming that one doesn't develop any dangerous superstitions, or has so many rituals that they become a real inconvenience, there's certainly nothing wrong with developing a routine that gives your mind and nerves a sense of contentment and reassurance. That's all good.

Why? Because every serious athlete is competitive about their game, and as one climbs the pyramid of competition, each step up pits one against other highly talented and highly competitive athletes. Besides, your opponent most likely is preparing for the game by relying on their own superstitions.

So in order to prepare and elevate your mind and body to a higher level, finding some way in your pregame preparation to make you feel good and confident may indeed come from your individual superstition.

## WILL SUPERSTITIONS GET YOU TO THE ZONE?

In short, the unspoken purpose of a superstition is that you are always trying to reach that "special space" in your game where you are doing everything well. It's that rare spot that athletes experience where, as is often said, "the game just seems to slow down" or "the pitch just seemed as big as a beach ball" or "the basket was as large as the ocean—I couldn't miss all night" or "I just found my game was on automatic pilot tonight … I was unconscious out there."

Chances are that on some occasions in your playing career, you too have found yourself elevated to this rarefied level. It's often called being "in the zone"—a term that has been around for several decades now, but has really become the domain of Dr. Mihaly Csikszentmihalyi, longtime professor and chairman of the Department of Psychology at the University of Chicago.

In his years of study, not only has Dr. Csikszentmihalyi formalized this sense of optimal performance, but his notable work has made athletes (as well as other performers, surgeons, pilots, and anyone who has to be on top of their game) aware that the very best performances come from when one is in this heightened state.

But here's the problem with being in the zone: It tends to be only temporary. Like the wind, it just comes and goes. Even worse, there's no set formula as to how to get one into the zone. Some days, you're just locked in, and you just feel you're totally in charge of the game. You don't hear the crowd noise or any other distractions. You aren't aware of the weather conditions or any pain or if you're hungry. In fact, you really aren't aware of your opponent. All you know—and feel—is that everything you want to do during the game is under your total control, and that you seemingly call the shots.

As you know, this is a simply wonderful feeling. You are 100 percent confident. There is no sense of any worry or anxiety. You control all of your actions at such a superior level that you can't help but be the star that day.

Over the years, and as a former professional athlete myself, I used to wonder how I could develop a pregame pattern that would aid me to get into this elusive zone. And even better, once I got there, how could I make sure I stayed there?

By the way, if you still aren't sure what I mean by the "zone" let me try this approach. Have you ever become so totally involved in a demanding task, like taking an important test in school, that suddenly, you looked up and realized that time has passed quickly without your even being aware of it? Perhaps the test started at 1 p.m., and you were so caught up in writing down the answers to the exam that you glanced at your watch and see that it's now 3 p.m.

Or maybe you've been playing a video game, and you've become so absorbed in keeping up with the action on the screen that you lose track of all time around you and when you finally take a moment to pause and to take a break, you are surprised that an hour has passed without your being aware of it.

That feeling of concentrating so much that you aren't aware of the passage of time means you've been in the zone. As many athletes observed, it's as though your mind was on automatic pilot. It's almost as though you lost a sense of awareness of true consciousness.

Of course, this is all something of an exaggeration, but if anything, when you are in the zone, you are actually even more acutely conscious than normal. Most athletes play at a normal, everyday level of consciousness. That's to be expected. But when a pitcher is totally locked in, throwing strike after strike, hitting the corners with precision with each pitch, or a shooter finds that he's got a hot hand, and no matter where he shoots from on the court, he just *knows* the ball is going to hit nothing but net, that's being in the zone. And for those in the zone, you are *so* focused into that higher sense of consciousness, you just aren't aware of any outside distractions.

Again, as noted, it's a great place to be. So great, in fact, that I have never encountered an athlete who didn't aspire to be in the zone.

## WHAT THE ZONE IS NOT

Being in the zone is not to be confused with being relaxed or loose or just feeling good. Or for that matter, being so relaxed that you almost feel as though you're going to gently fall asleep. While relaxation is certainly part of reaching one's zone, simply being calm and feeling good during a game doesn't necessarily mean you're on automatic pilot. There's a real difference.

In fact, some athletes who are gearing up for a game actually become worried if they feel too loose or too relaxed during their warm-ups. While it might outwardly appear to fans and coaches that they are loose, deep down, they know that they need to step up their focus and sense of awareness since their body isn't feeling nervous. (I'll have more on this worrisome condition in the section on dealing with pregame jitters, and how top athletes actually look forward to that feeling, rather than trying to escape from it.)

Everybody wants to be in the zone. That's a given. But again, the hard truth is that no one has ever come up with a set formula or "can't miss" approach that guarantees that one can get there. That's why superstitious rituals have become so popular over the years. Deep down, athletes hope that by following the same pregame routine, somehow that behavior will lift them into the zone for that game.

In other words, it's the best one can do to theoretically ensure that he or she will have an excellent game, and even better, maybe even lift them to the zone. After all, the more often you can get into the zone, the better you're going to play.

But while to me superstitions are fine, the conscious and scientific mind knows that, deep down, superstitions clearly don't have a solid "cause and effect" on athletic performance. I don't think they can hurt. I also know that superstitions really don't have any long-lasting staying power.

## THE MAN BEHIND "THE ZONE"

Let me come back to the one person who is credited the most with his research on what the zone is, and what that experience is like. Dr. Mihaly Csikszentmihalyi's decades of research in this area are the gold standard when it comes to those individuals who want to be in the zone.

In the world of sports, you'll find that everyone from former Dallas Cowboys head coach Jimmy Johnson to former University of Arizona head baseball coach Jerry Stitt admire and embrace Dr. C's observations. In his classic book, *Flow: The Psychology of Optimal Experience*, he wrote: "One of the most frequently mentioned dimensions of the flow experience is that, while it lasts, one is able to forget all the unpleasant aspects of life. This feature of flow is an important by-product of the fact that enjoyable activities require a complete focusing of attention on the task at hand—thus leaving no room in the mind for irrelevant information."

For anyone has been in the zone, you already know what a glorious feeling it is to be there. Problem is, no one has figured out a way to get back into the zone on a regular basis.

This is why I believe so many athletes have developed pregame rituals, or superstitions. These are performed in the fervent hope that a repetition of one's previous actions will lift one's game back to the zone. As noted, Jerry Stitt, as quoted in an interview in *Collegiate Baseball* (February 12, 2016), acknowledges that it's key for ballplayers to get back into the zone, but that it's difficult. When Stitt had a hitter who was in a real nice groove at the plate, Stitt would insist that the player should not relax but rather work even harder at his hitting. Said Stitt: "My way of thinking is that when they are on top of their game is the time to work the hardest. You want to stay on top by making sure everything is just right."

Stitt continues: "In baseball you have the flow experience when you are in total rhythm with the pitcher and with the ball and see the ball big and don't even feel what your body is doing. A lot of times, you will hit the ball, and you won't even feel the contact. Everything seems to work perfectly."

That's about as good a description you will find of a hitter in the zone. Continuing on with Stitt's observations about the relationship between superstitions and getting into the zone: "I think superstitions play a big role in the flow experience. All the really good hitters have a definite routine they go through. It's not so much that the routine has anything to do with their hitting except getting them into that mental state that they want to be in prior to hitting."

It doesn't take much of a leap to see how pregame mannerisms and rituals, aka superstitions, play into the mental preparation of top players. One can even draw a very strong conclusion that perhaps top athletes do indeed focus on pregame individualized preparations which, they hope, will lift them into the zone during the upcoming game.

Remember, it's not just athletes who go through customized pre-performance rituals. The same preparation is commonplace with musicians, stage actors, surgeons, and so on. Anyone who has to perform for a concentrated period of time wants to be in the zone, and this is all seen as normal procedure. You can call it pregame preparation, or superstitions, but in the end, the ultimate goal is to get into the zone.

So while to me, having superstitions is fine, the conscious, rational, and scientific mind knows that, deep down, superstitions clearly don't have a solid cause and effect on athletic performance. Yet I don't think they can hurt. I also know that superstitions really don't have any long-lasting staying power.

All that being said, if superstitions do somehow play a role in helping one get into the zone, then it certainly makes sense to pursue them.

So if the ideal athletic stage is to be in the zone, is there a more consistent way to get there, despite relying on superstitions?

Perhaps. Read on.

# 3

# "SEEING" YOURSELF SUCCEED

BACK IN THE EARLY 1970S, there was a story making the rounds about an American soldier who had been captured during the Vietnam War, and was held captive for years. In order to maintain his sanity from the depressing and mind-numbing daily routine of being a prisoner of war, this particular soldier, who happened to be an avid golfer, would take the time each day to play his favorite hometown golf course *in his mind*. He would close his eyes in his cell, and then visualize in vivid and accurate detail each tee, each approach shot, and each putt.

He did this, day after day, to the point where, upon his eventual return to the United States some years later, he went to his local golf course, and went out and played his very best round of golf ever—even though he hadn't physically played a round in years. Not surprisingly, his friends and buddies were stunned and amazed: after all, this war veteran hadn't picked up a golf club since being sent overseas, and now, with no practice, he goes out and plays his best round ever.

When asked to explain how he was able to do this, the story, goes, he simply said: "Because I've been rehearsing this round of golf, every hole and every day in my head for years."

Now, the truth is, no researcher has been able to definitively pinpoint who this soldier was. And chances are that the story may have a grain of truth to it, but is probably exaggerated. But that really isn't the point. It's more about the potential power of visualization, and the story is strong enough and compelling enough that most athletes fully believe in this process of mind over body.

Then, in the classic book entitled *In Pursuit of Excellence* by Terry Orlick, which was first published in 1980, he lent even greater credence to this approach. Orlick, one of the first mainstream sports psychologists in this country, wrote: "Athletes who make the fastest progress and those who ultimately become their best make extensive use of performance imagery."

It all makes a lot of sense. And it wasn't too long before athletes from a variety of sports began to utilize visualization techniques, whether they were figure skaters who wanted to master a particular daunting part of their on-ice routine, gymnasts who desired to be perfect in their performances, or even Olympic divers.

These days, every sport psychologist knows about and preaches the value of visualization. But back when I was in college, and sports psychology was at an embryonic stage, visualization was not used or even known in the world of sports. As noted earlier, my own introduction to the concept came not from a sports psych book, but rather from a surgeon who wrote about how he mentally prepared to perform delicate operations.

Dr. Maxwell Maltz went through his own "pregame" ritual in which he lay down on a bed in a dark and quiet room, with no music or any other disturbances. Then, as his mind and body began to relax and his breathing calmed down, he would mentally rehearse every step of the upcoming surgery. He would lie very still, but in his head, he would visualize in vivid detail the operating room, the medical instruments, his associates, then the area where the incision would be made, and so on.

Step by step, and very slowly, he would "see" in his mind every crucial part of the operation, from beginning to end. Once the procedure was completed in his mind, Dr. Maltz would "wake up" from this visualization exercise, and he knew that he was now ready to perform the surgery in real life. For him, since he had already done operation in his head, now it was just a matter of doing it again—almost as though he were on automatic pilot.

In other words, he employed visualization techniques as a way to elevate his surgical skills to a higher level of concentration. Clearly, this "mental rehearsal" approach makes sense for athletes who want to do more than just rely on superstitions in order to get them "psyched and ready" for a game. I know by the time I was playing pro baseball, I made it a point each day of finding a quiet, dark room where I could visualize my upcoming performance in that night's game.

Of extreme importance in this exercise is that you must see yourself performing well. That is, you never visualize that you're overcoming a struggle, or fighting against yourself—just the opposite. For example, if you have been working hard to make an important physical adjustment to your game, this is the time to focus on seeing that new adjustment working flawlessly in your game. *See yourself succeed.* That's important and essential.

After about twenty to thirty minutes of doing your pregame visualization, you should get up, feeling refreshed, and most importantly, feel confident and prepared for the game. You don't need to talk about it or brag about your expectations for that game. Just know that, deep inside you, you now carry a sense of being mentally ready for action.

Does visualization guarantee that you will reach the zone in your upcoming game? No. But in my experience with athletes who practice visualization on a routine basis and make it part of their pregame setup, you do begin to feel that you are going to be lucky enough to be in the zone for that game. I'm convinced that feeling of confidence, of inner power, or being totally ready to perform comes from your visualization sessions.

## WHAT HAPPENS TO YOU AND YOUR BODY WHEN YOU VISUALIZE

If you are doing visualization properly, you will begin to gradually notice the power of your mind, and how it really does control all of your muscles, nerves, and emotions.

What I mean by that is as you lay quietly on your bed in a dark room, with no noise or outside distractions (that means no iPod playing music or television playing in the background), you need to focus on only those aspects of your upcoming game in a positive way. You close your eyes and start to see in your mind's eye yourself taking the field, or the court, or the diamond. You see yourself in third person—as if you were watching yourself from a front row seat, or on a television screen.

You can see the quiet determination on your face. You can see your calm resolve. You see yourself confidently going through your pregame stretching exercises. And you see all of this is in full-color, high definition scope.

Then you watch yourself as the game begins. You're making all the plays flawlessly. If you're a baseball pitcher, you're making all the right pitches to certain key spots around the plate. You have total command of your breaking pitches. Your mechanics are fluid and smooth. You see yourself totally in command. You see yourself succeeding, doing well, and enjoying yourself.

If you're a basketball player, you're handling the ball with ease. You're getting open for your shots, and you're shooting the ball with total focus on the basket. You see the ball going through the net with a swish. You feel that you have the hot hand. This is your night to shine, that you can't miss.

You go through the entire game, seeing the other team in their uniforms as well, and again, taking in the entire scene in vivid color. Why? Because the more you can convince your brain that what you are "seeing" is actually real, the more your brain will begin to take over. As you're visualizing all of this, you will also find that *your body is following your brain.*

That means as you "play" the game in your mind's eye, it is to be expected that you will feel an adrenaline rush go through your system as you "see" yourself making a big play. You might even discover that some of your leg or arm muscles will contract or twitch as you play the game in your head. Your breathing might become quicker to match the pace of the game. In some cases, you may even rise from your visualization session having perspired a bit.

This is all good.

It means that your body has responded to what your brain has experienced. Your body doesn't have the ability to distinguish from what is real and what is simply being imagined. So as you see yourself perform well during a visualization session, your body simply follows along: your hands may be wet from perspiration, your heartbeat has risen, a shot of adrenaline has coursed through your system, and so on. It's not uncommon to arise from your twenty-minute visualization session feeling that you just played a magnificent game.

But that's the point. You have mentally "trained" your body and your muscles to have played, and played well. That's what visualization is attempting to accomplish. To get your mind and your body totally lined up in order to play a terrific game.

## TODD HERMAN'S "ALTER-EGO" APPROACH

There are certainly other approaches to building one's sense of self-confidence. For example, I know that Todd Herman, who also considers Harvey Dorfman to have been a key influence in his career in working with top athletes, advocates the concept of designing an "alter-ego" for oneself. For those athletes who may find themselves being held back in reaching their most competitive level in games, Todd advocates that one develop a kind of separate personality, or alter-ego, that one can figuratively step into as one prepares for the upcoming contest.

It's an interesting psychological device, and one worth considering if you find that you are being held back from reaching your potential. For example, you might find you're doing great during practice sessions, but in the game, for some unknown reason, you don't enjoy the same level of success as you do in practice. Herman suggests devising a different make-believe "you" that will allow you to succeed during the games.

Like myself, Todd is a big believer in the work of Dr. Maltz, and when I spoke with Todd not too long ago, we both agreed that *Psycho-Cybernetics* was one of the seminal works in the field of visualization and in raising one's performance to a higher level.

## WHERE MUSCLE MEMORY FITS IN

This is the payoff of visualization. Your mind has "seen" you play at the top of your game, and your body has responded as though everything was real. Perhaps you have heard the term *muscle memory*. This pregame visualization process is a major part of muscle memory, as your brain is quietly reinforcing to your voluntary muscles what they need to do in order to return you to the top of your game.

As with any other habit, you are "training" your voluntary muscles to rise from an uncomfortable or perhaps awkward and conscious approach to becoming automatic, or subconscious. Let me give you an example to clarify.

There was once a time in your life when you weren't able to drive an automobile. Like most teenagers, you had to learn how to get behind the wheel of a car and figure how to steer it, which probably felt a little awkward. It probably took some time for you to get a real feel, or sense, of how to control the wheel. Then you had to coordinate your foot pressing on the gas pedal or on the brake while, of

course, steering the car. All in all, putting all of this together probably took some time for you to become truly comfortable.

Now, of course, these days, you hardly give any of these actions
any conscious thought at all. You get in the driver's seat, fire up the
engine and you're off. You never give a moment's thought about how
to use the steering wheel or try to figure out how to accelerate or
slow down. It's all become automatic to your brain.

It was the same process at work when you first sat down at a
computer keyboard and had to learn how to type. Chances are that
process took a little time to master—to know where the "q" key or
where the "any" key is, as in, "press any key." But within a few weeks
or so, you trained yourself so that you didn't have to literally stop and
search for the appropriate keys anymore—as you type, your hands
have now become automatically trained to know what you want to
type.

Let's say you're a baseball player. You have taken thousands of
swings with a bat, but now you have been told by a batting coach
that you need to somehow get the "hitch" or "loop" out of your
swing. Problem is, your arms and body are accustomed to that hitch,
because you have done it for years, and the swing has become "automatic" for you.

But now, you need to re-program your swing motion slowly
in order to re-teach and re-train those muscles to eliminate that
hitch. You work on it in batting practice, you videotape your swing,
and slowly, the hitch goes away. But you also know that, during the
course of game-time stress, you sometimes revert to that hitch.

That's where visualizing yourself without that hitch can really
make a tremendous difference. You are training your mind as well
as the muscles in your arms, shoulders, and wrists to learn to swing
the bat without that loop. That's the essence of muscle memory. You
are reprogramming your swing in such a way that you have not only
eliminated a negative part of your swing, but done it in a manner
that, both physically and psychologically, it has now become a subconscious, or automatic, part of your swing.

Does this muscle memory happen overnight? No, it doesn't. But once you start to pinpoint the exact problem you want to correct, and once you physically and mentally focus on how you want to improve upon that problem, that's the first step to using visualization and muscle memory to your advantage as an athlete, no matter what sport you play.

## THE BODY FOLLOWS THE BRAIN'S DICTATES

I can recall getting up from a twenty-minute visualization pregame session and realizing that my palms were sweaty and that I was totally psyched up—ready to rock 'n' roll due to the adrenaline rush I had experienced while "watching" my personal highlight reel, "seeing" myself doing everything right. Even though I had merely lay down on a bed and was "dreaming" all my actions in my brain, my physical body couldn't tell the difference between what was real and what was simply imagined. As far as my body's voluntary muscles were concerned, it was as though I had just completed a thorough workout.

But here's the key to making visualization—and the subsequent muscle memory—work.

You have to do it on a regular basis. It should become part of your daily routine. Just doing it a few times is not going to have the desired outcome you want. Just as we discussed earlier about how athletes focus a lot on training their bodies on a daily basis, the same is needed for your mental game, especially if you are in the process of attempting to re-train some well-ingrained habits.

Even more, you have to really focus hard on what you want to do correctly in your adjustments. Repetition is the absolute key here.

Here's the takeaway: The body follows the mind's dictates. Once you actively train your mind as to what you want to achieve, your body will follow along.

# VISUALIZATION AND PRACTICE=TO THE ZONE!

What you want to do is visualize your best and most effective actions in a game. Find these by pinpointing them from watching yourself do well on video, and then "burn" them into your mind.

Then, when you practice, be sure to keep that "perfect video" in your head as you go about your activities. The more you practice, and the more you keep that in your mind, the more automatic your actions will become. And when you reach a point in your games when you are playing on "automatic pilot," the better and more fluid your game will become.

What's the ultimate payoff? There are some who say that the more your competitive game becomes more of an automatic action, the closer you are to being in that much-desired "zone" where the game seemingly slows down and everything just seems that much easier.

# WHAT ABOUT BEING NERVOUS?

One of the most famous studies in psychology dates from the early twentieth century and is often cited in texts as the Yerkes-Dodson Law. Based upon the research of two Harvard psychologists, their theory was that humans perform their best when they are at the middle point between emotions. That is, if they are totally and fully relaxed, they will not perform at a top optimal level. But on the other hand, if they are totally stressed out at the other extreme, that will also get in their way of their best performance. In short, they concluded that in order to achieve peak performance, an individual has to be somewhere in between those two extremes of emotions.

For decades, the Yerkes-Dodson principle was been accepted as being the gospel in terms of how to prepare for a major competition, test, performance, whatever. But then in the 1970s, a Finnish psychologist named Yuri Hanin began to challenge that so-called psychological law. Hanin found that lots of top Finnish and other

European athletes actually performed well when they reported feeling high levels of stress.

In short, Hanin showed that those feeling full-level stress—along with other emotions—actually performed better. True, the results varied from athlete to athlete, but overall, the athletes who did well in preparing for competitions discovered that by using their stress to pinpoint their Individualized Zone of Optimal Functioning (IZOF), they often found themselves closer to reaching the magical zone, i.e., that area of full absorption into accomplishing one's goals.

Over the years, the IZOF model has been adapted and modified, but it's one of the few psychological approaches that acknowledge that many athletes actually thrive on stress, and as a consequence, they do not need to run away from it, or try to eliminate it. If anything, they want to embrace it.

In other words, don't be afraid or back off from being nervous in a tight situation. Actually, you should look forward to it because it means you are that much closer to getting into the zone. The irony is that when you are in the zone, it may feel as though you are totally relaxed. But in order to achieve that level of optimal performance, you need to build upon your visualization techniques, be confident in your skill level and subsequent nervousness, and rely upon your pregame rituals and superstitions in the hope that the combination of all will get you to where you want to be.

## DOES MUSCLE MEMORY STAY WITH YOU?

When it comes to the long-lasting impact of muscle memory, consider this: There's a terrific television commercial for New York Life that features NBA Hall of Famer Rick Barry shooting his traditional underhanded free throws. The commercial shows Barry, now in his early seventies, hitting his shots just as easily and as accurately as when he was playing in the NBA and shooting free throws—underhanded—with 90 percent accuracy. And then, just to drive home the point, he puts on a blindfold and takes his stance on the free throw line.

What happens? As you might imagine, he sinks his next free throw easily.

How is that possible? Because Rick's made so many free throws in his life that by now, he just trusts his instincts and muscle memory to take over all the combined physical actions of arms, legs, hands, fingers, wrists—pretty much everything that goes into making an underhanded free throw.

If you haven't seen the TV commercial, just Google it, and you'll see a perfect example of the power of muscle memory through practice and repetition. Just imagine—hitting one's free throws blindfolded. That's the ultimate in visualization.

## A NEW BREAKTHROUGH VIA COMPUTER TRAINING VIDEOS?

With the rise in popularity of sabermetrics in baseball, and with analytics spreading into pretty much all of the mainstream popular sports, there has been a subsequent and not unexpected rise in whether the actual performance of an athlete can be enhanced as well. No, I'm not talking about performance-enhancing drugs, which have been proven to add more muscle and strength, or to increase one's level of concentration, or to add a little pep and push into one's game. Of course, all of these performance-enhancing techniques have been outlawed.

And I should also point out that I'm not talking about the interesting neurological breakthroughs in the scientific world in, say, what's the precise medical explanation for a major-league hitter to recognize whether an incoming 90 mph pitch is a strike or a ball, or whether it's a good pitch to swing at. While the physiological studies in this area are definitely fascinating, at the end of the day, the truth is, there really isn't much practical takeaway of application for hitters. All that remains from these kinds of studies in recent years is that the hitter still only has a split second to make the decision to swing or to take the pitch. Researchers do, of course, anticipate that more years of work and analysis will help find out more about the brain's processing of this kind of rapid-fire decision-making, but such real-world applications are years and years away.

But what I want to focus on here are a number of new initiatives which are designed to help train and improve one's visual or physical approach to one's sport. The hard truth is that I'm not aware of any innovation or new kind of approach that is guaranteed to help an athlete get into the zone. Yes, there are new computer-based video games that are being promoted as systems that will help enhance an athlete's reaction time, or to perhaps train and expand and sharpen one's peripheral vision. But there are two major reasons to be a little wary: one, even the most advanced technologies in this area still haven't been proven to work, and two, as creative as these new systems are, they still focus primarily on the physical components of an athlete's makeup, with the hope that greater self-confidence in one's ability will help improve their overall game.

Don't get me wrong. I applaud these efforts. We're always looking for new ways to improve one's game. But let me quote: "As *The New York Times* reported this year, there remains a considerable degree of skepticism among scientists and researchers about the benefit of cognitive training. Teams and individuals across a variety of sports continue to invest substantial sums—and even more faith—in systems claiming to hone the mind."

The article continues: "Some experts retain the suspicion, however, that they are being sold a myth, that for all the advanced graphics and bold claims, computer programs designed to improve mental performance are, at best, a harmless placebo and, at worse, an expensive delusion." (*New York Times*, March 5, 2017.)

In other words, I think we all agree that it would be simply wonderful if a computer program or video game could be invented that would propel athletes to their top level of performance for each game. After all, such an approach would most likely be quicker, more inviting, and more fun than having to go through the somewhat difficult, and at times painful, self-reflection process of writing out a mental cue card, or coming to grips with one's poor performance in a game, or how to make difficult adjustments, or taking the time to prepare for an upcoming game to visualize. But as the article reveals, the new computer-based neurological programs have not been proven to work all the time.

Yet, despite these negative critiques and the expense, video programs such as NeuroTracker and CogniSens continue to grow in popularity. Again, I can understand why young athletes can become attracted to these "training" sessions: they're derived from video games, which most athletes today grew up on, and again, who wouldn't want to improve their game by simply doing these sessions? In a rough analogy, it's like saying that if you want to lose weight, instead of having to hit the gym and getting on the treadmill every day for weeks on end, why not opt for a video program that is fun, enjoyable, and gets you to lose weight quickly? The fact that there is no hard scientific evidence to prove weight loss doesn't seem to be taken into consideration.

"I have to be extremely skeptical of any training program that promotes the development of these generic visual, perceptual, cognitive functions," says A. Mark Williams, chairman of the department of the health, kinesiology, and recreation at the University of Utah (*New York Times*, January 8, 2017).

This is not a minority viewpoint. In a publication entitled *Psychological Science in the Public Interest* (October 2016), and cited in the *New York Times* article, a number of researchers concluded that: "the evidence was 'limited and inconsistent' that commercial brain-training software could enhance cognition outside the laboratory in the ways the companies described."

What's the bottom line? At this juncture, only you, the athlete, can decide whether this kind of "mental training" is effective for you. And it might be. But as of today, the overwhelming evidence is that there is little conclusive proof that so-called training programs can really help. Here's hoping that, someday, all of this scientific research will result in some major—and practical—applications, but as for today, as an athlete, it's important to live by the motto of *caveat emptor*, i.e., buyer beware.

If you'd like a more detailed, academic account of how to make significant adjustments to one's skills, I would refer you to an article entitled "Implementing the Five-A Model of Technical Refinement: Key Roles of the Sports Psychologist" by Howie J. Carson and Dave Collins, in the *Journal of Applied Psychology*, Volume 28, Number 4, 2016, pp. 392–409). In their article, the authors break down long-range adjustment of established athletic skills through five stages: Analysis, Awareness, Adjustment, (Re) Automation, and Assurance. A good deal of this "re-training" relies upon the athlete studying videotape of their actions, working in conjunction with the sports psychologist.

# 4

# THE SLIPPERY SLOPE OF SETTING GOALS

IN MY READINGS OF SPORTS psychology how-to manuals over the years, invariably one of the first chapters states that the athlete should learn how to set individual goals for oneself before the season begins. In other words, in order to prepare for a great season, you need to first map out a set of goals that are achievable.

The theory behind goal-setting is that unless you know where you want to go before you start, you run a serious risk of getting lost along the way and not reaching your target. As a result, many athletes go through the mental exercise before the season begins of writing down what they fully expect their stats for the year to be.

In sum, it seems like a nice and neat way to plan ahead for success, and of course, to put a certain level of expectation on the athlete to shoot for.

But from my experience with athletes, while goal-setting may seem like a straightforward approach, I often worry about those individuals who set lofty goals for themselves—but then find those goals are either *too* lofty or just flat-out unrealistic. Even worse, about a third or so into the season, they discover that since they can't reach those goals, they become discouraged and privately start to give up on the rest of the year.

In other words, they have needlessly put themselves into a depression because the goals they set have proven to be too much of a reach.

From my perspective, this all sounds so unnecessary. Why put that kind of extra pressure on yourself? It's hard enough to compete and try to do well on a daily basis. So why add to that pressure? Sure, everybody dreams about having a breakout year, and becoming a superstar. But if you start piling on all sorts of milestones and goals on yourself, you're not going to go very far before you realize most of your targets are not going to be met. And that realization only eats away at your self-confidence.

Let me give you an example. Back in the early 1990s, the Cleveland Indians' first-round draft choice was a young outfielder out of George Washington High School in New York City. Manny Ramirez, originally from the Dominican Republic, was truly a gifted hitter. His wrist strength and bat speed were remarkable.

I first met Manny just after he had signed and was playing in low Class A ball in North Carolina. A fairly quiet and shy kid, he was of course eager to get off to a good start in his pro career. And by all accounts, he was doing fine in his first few weeks. While he wasn't tearing the cover off the ball, he was giving every indication that he had rare and unique ability to hit.

But then one day, I recall Manny and I were talking in the outfield during batting practice. The then nineteen-year-old was concerned. He explained that in high school, no matter where he had played, he had always hit for a very high batting average. I seem to recall in his senior year he hit well over .600, which was particularly impressive since every team he played against knew how good he was, plus every game there was a flock of big-league scouts in attendance to watch him perform.

Yet here in pro ball, it was a different story. Manny was hitting somewhere around .250, as I remember, and this was a whole new experience for him. He knew that, as a first-round draft choice, there were major expectations in front of him. And yet, for some reason—in his mind—he was struggling.

We began to talk. For starters, whereas back in New York City, his high school team played only a few times a week, here in pro ball, you played games seven days a week. The only days off came from rainouts. For a new player, having games every night adds a certain level of daily expectation that most young players—especially first-round draft choices—have a difficult time coming to terms with.

In short, Manny was concerned about how he was going to live up to his goal of hitting .300 for the season. From his perspective, that's what was expected of him from the Indians, and as such, that became his goal. But as he explained to me, so far in his short career, one night he would get two hits, but the next night he might go hitless, and then the next night he would go 1-for-4.

For a kid who was accustomed to always collecting two or three hits in every game he played, this up-and-down track record was very stressful to him. It was something that he had never experienced before.

I suggested a different kind of goal-setting to Manny.

"Let me ask you this. You've seen the pitching in this league. Are the guys hittable here? Or do you think you're over your head?"

Manny nodded his head that the guys he was facing were definitely hittable.

"OK, so let's look at a week of games. I know that you didn't play a game every day in high school, but here of course, you are. The front office in Cleveland knows that the best way to get you to progress is to get as many at-bats in a game as possible in order to keep getting better.

"But I also recognize that the front office, as well as you, is keeping track of your batting average. But if you take a long-range approach to an entire minor-league season, and promise yourself that you're going to hit over .300, that can be hard to visualize because, it seems, you're on a mental see-saw. That is, one day you're feeling good because you got a couple of hits, but the next day, you're down because you went hitless."

Manny listened, and I continued.

"So let me suggest this. Forget trying to set a long-term goal for the entire season. Let's just focus instead on a week-by-week approach. In other words, break your long-range goals into a series of more reasonable goals. In other words, if you play a full week of games, and you get up, say, four times a game, that means you will get up twenty-eight or thirty times a week, correct?

"Then, let me ask you this. If you get thirty at-bats in a week of games, can you get ten hits during that span?

Manny smiled. "Ten hits in thirty at-bats? Sure, that shouldn't be a problem."

(Note to reader: Please remember this is Manny Ramirez, one of the greatest hitters of all time. He wasn't being cocky or bragging; he was just being honest, or as fans like to say, Manny being Manny.)

So I suggested that Manny make his short-term goal to collect ten hits a week. I urged him to forget about the ups and downs of his daily performances, where one day he might get just one hit, and the next day he might go hitless. Rather, he should focus on the entire week's collection of hits. If he could get just ten hits, he would be doing just great.

It was a mental approach to hitting that he had never considered before.

And judging from his lifetime batting average both in the minors and majors, Manny seems to have done fine.

But my overall point is this: Manny was being burdened and weighed down by this long-range goal of wanting to hit .300 or better for an entire season in the minors. That goal can be overwhelming, especially if you get off to a slow start. After a while, it's all you think about, and that kind of goal pressure just isn't needed.

A better and more efficient approach is to break up any goals you might have into smaller, bite-sized chunks that not only are more realistic in their expectations, but also won't be so overwhelming in their long-range scope.

# 5

# DEALING WITH PREGAME JITTERS

A YOUNG ATHLETE REPORTS THAT he or she becomes so tense and nervous before a game that they can't relax—that their breathing accelerates and ratchets up, and that they need some way to gain control of their pregame anxiety.

Some even report that they get so fired up that they discover that their hands and fingers are literally shaking with anticipation. This is often one of the biggest issues confronting sports psychologists.

Confession: I used to be like that. I would get so amped before a big game in high school that my hands would tremble and shake from pure nervous anxiety. I had no idea why this would happen, but it did. I would search high and low for some way to get my body to calm down and relax. I read self-help manuals from psychologists who advocated that in order to be able to reach a pinnacle of performance I needed to rope in my anxieties.

Most of those manuals said to control my breathing by taking deep and controlled breaths. Big slow inhale ... hold it for a few seconds ... then exhale it slowly. Oh, and along with every deep exhale, I was supposed to imagine that my nervous energy was being dissipated into space by my deep release. And that I should repeat that several times. Unfortunately, this deep breath–and–release approach didn't work for me.

Other books suggested that I was merely hyperventilating, and that I should grab a small paper bag and breathe into it so that the combination of oxygen and carbon dioxide would calm me down. I tried that a few times as well, and didn't see much of an improvement.

Another approach I heard was to get pregame jitters under control by designing a "calm and safe place" in my head where the ongoing and lasting image was always one of being serene and confident. The idea was that if I worked hard to create such a place in my mind, I could go there whenever I felt tense and anxious.

But here's the problem.

None of those approaches ever worked for me. No matter how hard I tried to breathe out the bad nervousness, or to think only positive and reassuring thoughts, it never seemed to work. It seemed as though I was destined to have to deal with these pregame issues. And by the way, I had read about top athletes who also talked about being nervous before a game, but once the game began, the anxiety seemed to suddenly disappear. Here again, that wasn't the case with me. I found that my nerves would carry over into the game for the first few minutes before I began to calm down. But eventually, once I was caught up in the game's flow, I was fine.

But then one day, I was relating all of these pregame jitters to my father, Bob Wolff, who, as a sportscaster, enjoyed such a spectacular career of calling major sporting events on-air that he's been honored by both the baseball and basketball Halls of Fame. I asked Dad how he dealt with the nervous anxiety that built up in his system before he went on the air before calling a World Series or NFL Championship game. And his answer surprised me.

"Rick, I learned a long time ago that I never wanted to lose those feelings of being edgy," he told me. "Because when I was feeling nervous, I realized that was my body's way of telling me that it was now ready for me to be on top of my game ... that I was totally focused ... and that I was ready to go.

"To me, the worst thing that could happen to me is if I didn't get nervous. That to me would signal a real concern, as if my body were somehow deserting me. Being calm and relaxed before a performance was the last thing I wanted. I looked forward to being anxious. That was both a good and a reassuring sign to me."

I had never heard that philosophy before, and that approach made a lot of sense to me. And from that day forward, I counsel athletes to turn their pregame jitters around. Instead of trying to reduce the anxiety or eliminate it, they should simply try to embrace it. In other words, it should serve to be reassuring to you to know that your body and mind are getting wound up for the upcoming game. It's your body's way of telling you you're ready to perform.

And as noted, all of the pregame jitters will pass quietly once the game begins (in some cases, it might take a few plays for all to calm down). But don't worry—it will.

What's the takeaway here? Well, let's assume you've prepared yourself for the upcoming game with the following approaches:

1. You have made visualization techniques a daily part of your athletic ritual. Just as you hone your physical body with workouts, weight training, running, and practice, you also need to start fine-tuning your mind into what you want your body to do when you go out to compete. You need to start paying attention to the mental side of your approach if you want to compete, and compete well, at the next level.

2. The ultimate effect of visualization is that **you will begin to build up a sense of muscle memory** in your system, so that

you are now getting your physical body aligned with how you visualize your game being lifted to a higher level. Again, this process takes time ... weeks, months, and perhaps even longer. So the sooner you adapt this training regimen into your daily activity, the better and more consistent your game will become.

3. And yes, **you can keep your superstitions with you,** so long as they aren't getting in the way of the team, or of any teammate. And ideally, try to keep the superstitions to a minimum level. Remember, all they are providing is a kind of a security blanket so that you can lift your game into the zone.

4. Remember, **if you can find your way into the zone on a regular basis, you'll be a very happy competitor.** People describe being in the zone as "everything in the game just slowed down for me ... there were no outside distractions ... everything I wanted to do during the game came out perfectly, just as I had planned."

That, to me, would be the essence of one's mental game and physical game coming together in total sync at the right time. But there are still those moments when the athlete is caught up in a struggle to be too perfect. And that can cause performance issues.

## THE "PERFECT PITCH" SYNDROME

Trying too hard to be perfect can get in the way of your success. You have to focus on what got you here—not on changing your approach now.

When I was working for the Indians, one day I was called in by the front office to evaluate a trend they were noticing with their young, talented pitchers who were being called up from the minors to the big-league club.

In effect, these pitchers, who had been so good in either Triple A or Double A, suddenly were overmatched in the big leagues. Now, it's not uncommon for a young player to be a little intimidated when they make their debut in the big leagues, but in this case, the front office was suddenly seeing kids who had total and pinpoint control in the minors suddenly not being able to find the strike zone in the big leagues. Guys who routinely threw strikes to get ahead of the batters now were falling behind in the count and either walking them or just making themselves much more vulnerable to being hit hard.

It was baffling to all concerned. These young pitchers were clearly eager to please, their mechanics seemed solid, and yet, upon being promoted to the big leagues, they were no longer throwing consistent strikes. Even worse, the pitchers themselves couldn't figure it out: it was as though that upon reaching the pinnacle of their lifelong dreams—of being promoted to the major leagues—they just weren't good enough to perform well at this elite level.

I decided to spend a little time talking with one tall left-hander who was considered a top prospect.

I asked him for his assessment of what was going on. And I remember him telling me, "I have worked my tail off all my life to get to the big leagues, and now that I'm here, I'm doing everything I possibly can to make sure I'm perfectly sharp in my pitches. I don't want any screw-ups. I can't afford to make any bad pitches. If I do, I will have blown my opportunity, and my dream will be over."

The more I thought about his approach, the more I began to sense the amount of extreme pressure he had placed upon himself. He had made it clear to himself that he couldn't afford to make any mistakes. And therein lays the problem, or what I described as "the perfect pitch" syndrome. It's just what it sounds like: a healthy, young, and ambitious pitcher is so determined to shine in his big-league debut that he is going to make sure every pitch he throws is absolutely perfect in every way possible.

That, of course, is a most commendable goal.

The problem is, it's not very realistic. No matter how much we plan and try to be perfect in our performances, the reality is that being perfect is just not going to happen. Even worse, if you're a pitcher, and you're valiantly trying to throw not just strikes, but perfect strikes on the outside corner, or at the knees, you are most likely really going to struggle to walk that kind of mental tightrope. Even worse, because of your zeal in your quest for a perfect outing, you might discover that you are actually heading in the opposite direction. Instead of being 0-2 on the batter, you are now 2-0, and things are beginning to unravel quickly for you.

And then the downward spiral begins. Because of your quest to be so perfect, you end up walking the first batter you face, then you make a mistake to the next batter who lines a single, and then the next batter walks.

Instead of retiring the side with three strikeouts, you have the bases loaded and no one out. And you have no idea what you have done wrong.

Most young pitchers when faced with this kind of outing quickly become frazzled and lose their composure. "I had such good stuff in the bullpen and was certain I was going to be able to hit my spots perfectly in the game. What happened?"

What happened is that you set *too* high a standard in trying to be perfect. A better approach would have been to simply try and do one's best to be perfect *but* if you miss by a little, that's OK. Don't make the fatal mistake of beating yourself up about it. Rather, accept the imperfect pitch and force yourself focus only on the next one. Striving to be *too* perfect all the time will cause more heartaches than just relying on your athletic skills and mental preparation to take you where you want to go.

Bear in mind that these young pitchers had all dominated during their minor-league careers and had never experienced this kind of emotional overload before where they felt that they had to be perfect on the mound. They had pitched with confidence in the minors, and knew how to focus on throwing strikes, and then fooling the batters with breaking balls and changeups. But somehow, when they attained the highest rung on the ladder, they suddenly felt that there was no room for an error—that they had to be perfect on every single pitch. And that pressing desire for perfection got directly in the way of their success.

As I talked more with the young lefty pitcher, he began to see what had been holding him back. He agreed that while he certainly wanted to perform well in his next outing, he couldn't mentally defeat himself if he delivered a pitch that wasn't perfect. And if he did make a mistake or two, he needed to readjust and get himself back to what had worked for him in the minors.

This may sound like a very obvious adjustment, but trust me, making that psychological jump from the minors to the majors can be huge.

## GETTING ALL A'S ON YOUR REPORT CARD

Let me give you an analogy from the classroom. If you set a goal for yourself that you will not only achieve an A average in school, but that you must also achieve a grade of 100 on every test, exam, and final you take, well, you're setting a goal of total perfection for yourself.

Anything less than 100—perhaps a 97 or a 95, which is still exemplary and is still very much an A average—isn't good enough for you, since you're a perfectionist. After all, if your goal is to be perfect all the time in school, then while getting an answer or two wrong on an exam might not affect your overall A average, the truth is, it won't be 100 percent pure.

For many ambitious and competitive athletes, the same mindset is at work. They insist on throwing every pitch totally perfectly with no room for human error. Every at-bat has to be perfect. Every shot they take in a basketball game has to be perfectly executed. Every pass they throw as a quarterback has to be perfect. And so on.

But that's the key. We're all human. No matter how much we strive for total perfection in the classroom or in a competitive game, the reality is that we're just not going to be perfect all the time.

The downside is that when you don't achieve perfection, you feel as though you have failed and let yourself down.

Of course, from the other perspective, if you say to yourself, *Wow—I achieved straight A's this semester—that's pretty cool* regardless of whether you had grades of 92, 94, 95, and so on, that's a much healthier and more positive perspective. It shouldn't matter if you got all 100's. You still achieved all A's.

That same approach should be used with pitchers or any players playing in their first couple of big-league games. Rather than define their success or failure solely on whether they were perfect, it's much more productive to reflect after the game on everything they did well. Sure, there are bound to be some disappointing moments in the mix. But if your positive moments outweigh your negative ones, you're quietly beginning to build a sense of confidence of your game. And that's the key.

You have to always bear in mind that what got you to this level is not being too perfect, but doing what comes naturally to you. Mentally, by subconsciously shifting your approach to "being totally perfect," you have actually tilted the psychological approach that had worked so well for you in the minors. The bottom line is: you didn't try to throw perfect pitches in the minors—you just pitched to the best of your ability—so why are you trying to be perfect now in the big leagues?

It sounds like a simple question, but you'd be amazed how many eager rookies fall into this seemingly unexpected trap of trying to be perfect. Famed pitching coach Rick Peterson talks about this in his book *Crunch Time: How to Be Your Best When it Matters Most.* He had noticed over the years in working with big-league pitchers that too many of them, when faced with things going off the rails in the game, will simply "hump it up" and "try even harder."

As Rick points out, he actually counsels pitchers to "try less hard" when this happens. What he means is that we live in a society where competitors are told all the time that in order to succeed, they need to try that much harder when things get tough. Peterson points out the flaw in this assumption. What you really need to do is to *stay within your optimal arousal level* if you want to perform at your best. If you try too hard and push yourself too hard, you will not only mess up your mechanics, but in doing so, you will ultimately fail.

The bottom line? It's always better to stay within your limits and to perform at a level at which you are comfortable and not pushing too hard.

## THE FEAR OF SUCCESS/THE FEAR OF FAILURE

So is trying to be perfect in a gamer the same as, or comparable to, what is commonly known as a fear of failure?

Well, it's somewhat related to a fear of failure. But to me, it's more closely aligned to a fear of success.

Let me clarify and define, and you'll see what I mean:

In my perspective, *an athlete with a fear of success is someone who has already tasted a sense of success at the highest level, but now is being asked to go out and succeed again.* The desire for repeated success can unexpectedly place an unseen burden of expectation on the athlete.

That, to me, is the genesis of a fear of success—a taste of success, followed by pressure and expectation to go out and do it again and again. I did well the first time, so now people expect me to perform at a high level again and again. That's real pressure!

By contrast, an athlete with a fear of failure is someone who works exceedingly hard to improve their skills, but once game time arrives, they become somewhat paralyzed to go out and show their stuff.

Why? My sense is that they have worked so hard to get to this key point in their athletic career that they become overwhelmed at taking the next step.

It's almost as though they can't even bear the thought of going out and not doing well. What happens if I go out and am a total flop?

If that occurs, then from their viewpoint, all that work and effort has gone down the drain. When seen in that kind of drastic light, the athlete can suddenly find themselves unable to focus, or will show other signs of distraction, mainly because they are so worried about not succeeding.

It's as though all their inner demons and goblins of insecurity have joined forces at this very moment to try and sabotage their big moment in the sun.

As discussed earlier, some psychologists try to counteract this by giving the athlete some kind of chant or mantra that they can repeat over and over to themselves to counter the anxiety. Others suggest taking deep breaths, over and over again, in order to regulate one's breathing. Some sports psychologists will recommend that the athlete focus on positive thoughts, or going to their "happy place" in their head.

For some athletes, I guess that these kinds of quick fixes can help get them over the hump. But to me, despite their best efforts, they don't really address the core issue of a "fear of failure" to perform.

I believe it's much more advisable to get the athlete to focus on their fear of failure, e.g., that they are understandably nervous because this moment represents a big opportunity for them. At that point, let them just talk their anxiety out. Let them talk about what this opportunity means for them. Let them focus on all the good things that could follow. How much they have dreamed about this moment.

In other words, let them concentrate—and talk—about the positive.

But if they do start to then focus on what could go wrong, simply ask them: Do you have the talent? Have you worked hard? Do you deserve to succeed? Have you prepared to succeed?

In other words, gently but firmly guide them to remind themselves of how much *talent* they have and how *good* they are and *how much* they have put into their success. Eventually, they will begin to believe in the conversation, and will be much better prepared to concentrate on what they need to succeed. Get them to totally focus on what their mental approach should be and how to *trust* their body and mind to get them to where they want to go.

With an individual who is focused on a fear of success, it's important to have them review the video of their recent previous (and successful) performances. Let them view the video over and over again and allow them to bask in their success. As they begin to relax and smile, ask the athlete to talk about what they were feeling in the moment. Most often, he or she will talk about how good they were feeling, that they were confident at how well things were going, and that they were actually enjoying the moment. Don't be surprised if they even begin to smile.

Then, continue to get them to talk about their next game or event. Try to get them to carry over the warmth and confidence of their previous outing to the next one. Remind them how good and confident they felt with the first performance, and stress to them that the second go-round will actually be easier and seamless.

Why? Because not only have they enjoyed themselves, but that inner core of confidence has now been activated in them and that's the key sense of experience that all top athletes crave. Remember, you can't teach experience. But once you begin to accumulate it instinctively by performing in a game or event, then it's there and it can't be taken away. That's important.

As for the rookie neophyte who hasn't performed in a major spotlight for the first time, the emphasis in your conversation should focus on how much talent and drive they have exhibited to get to this point. Sure, there are expectations, and it's fine to recognize that. But the emphasis should be to get the athlete to think how good they are going to feel once their first outing is completed. And in order to ensure a good outcome, they need to focus on relying upon athletic instinct.

# THAT VOICE OF SELF-DOUBT THAT POPS UP DURING THE GAME

You know the feeling. And it's not a good one.

You've been working hard throughout the game, and yet, for reasons you can't explain, it's just not happening for you on this day. You're focused. You're on top of your game. And you're not tired.

But suddenly, that little voice of self-doubt begins to pop up in your head. *Hey, c'mon . . .it's OK to bail out. You've made a solid and thorough effort. It's just not your day*, the voice tells you. *So, don't sweat it … it just wasn't meant to be.*

Every athlete has heard that voice of defeat. It starts out in a very subtle manner, but in the end, it's telling you to justify your defeat . . . to rationalize why things didn't work today. And unfortunately, it's extremely hard to ignore that inner voice.

So what do you do? In my experience, those top athletes who simply try to ignore the voice of defeat end up becoming even more distracted from the task at hand. Why? Because they spend too much time trying to distract themselves psychologically, or waste too much mental effort attempting to suppress those negative thoughts.

I tell athletes that when that voice pops up, take a moment to confront it. Give it a few seconds to say what it has to tell you, and then confront it. *OK, I agree. I haven't been sharp today. Things aren't going the way I expected them to*. But that doesn't mean you give up and throw in the towel.

No, the opposite is true. This is the time to recognize that you need to make quick adjustments in your game. Be objective with yourself. Think through what isn't working well and then give yourself an internal evaluation on how you need to make corrections, adjustments, etc. to your game. Sometimes, it's just a small physical tinker. Others demand an overhaul of your original game plan.

But whatever the adjustment is, you need to start focusing on making those changes right away.

In effect—and I know this may sound odd—but having that little voice of self-doubt getting into your ear is a positive wake-up call that you need to start making adjustments now. The question is, of course, how does one make adjustments on the fly in the middle of a tough and heated contest?

# 6
# THE ROAD TO MAKING IN-GAME ADJUSTMENTS

So WHAT DO YOU DO when you're working your tail off on your game, but nothing seems to be working well? You're not in the zone, and yet, you've come into the game mentally and physically prepared.

You know you're in excellent shape, you have spent all sorts of extra hours on polishing and honing your skills, you feel good and confident about your game, and you're getting the opportunities to show your stuff.

But yet . . . it's just not happening in this game.

Let me give you some routine examples:

In basketball, your jump shot is off. Just this past week you were drilling 15-footers from all over the court during practice, swish after swish. But during the game, while you're getting good looks at the hoop, your shots are inexplicably hitting off the back rim.

In baseball, you're working hard every day in batting practice to hit pitches on the far side of the plate to the opposite field, and you've actually become very consistent at it, with line drive after line drive being hit the other way.

But during the game, when you do get a pitch on the far corner, you find yourself either popping them up or fouling the pitch back. No line drive to be found.

As a pitcher, you have tremendous command of your breaking ball in the bullpen. You feel great. You sense that opposing hitters won't be able to even sniff your pitches. But then you get to a point in the game where you're in a close spot, and suddenly, it seems that you've lost command of your pitches. You can't find the strike zone. Everything is high and soft in the strike zone. You find yourself falling behind in the count.

Suddenly, you're in a cold sweat on a hot night. That little voice of doubt is begging to nag at you—telling you that it's just not your night. No matter how hard you try to suppress that doubt, it keeps popping up.

There's probably no feeling in sports that is more frustrating. It's as though your mind and body just aren't paying attention to you or your preparation during the games.

So what do you do when things aren't going your way?

Does it help at all to feel sorry for yourself because you had a bad game? Well, if you're a member of the human species, you're definitely going to feel sorry for yourself. To me, that's to be expected. And quite honestly, it shows me that you care deeply about your performance. After all, if you didn't show any emotion of despair and sadness, that would get my attention, as in, "What's wrong with this guy? He just had a terrible game ... and he doesn't seem bothered by it."

In my experience, I would counsel athletes to give themselves some serious time after the game during which they do feel sorry for themselves. Not to feel down would be trying to repress real human emotion.

Here's the key. Feeling down and out is totally expected. *But how you then react to the bad game is what matters most.* You need to climb out of your well of self-pity by not so much giving yourself a pep talk, but rather trying to objectively evaluate what went wrong in your game that night. At the higher levels of athletic competition, you need to focus on what adjustments you tried to make in the game, and more importantly, why they didn't work. Without that candid and objective evaluation, you're not going to be able to lift your game or to get it back on track. This is what Harvey Dorfman was attempting to do when he confronted stars and told them it was their responsibility to look deep into their game and figure out on their own what had gone haywire.

As noted, a lot of sports psychologists or coaches will seem to view these self-talks as a kind of internal pep talk—as a motivational tool to encourage you not to give up, not to quit. Well, I guess that's fine. But to me, that's only like putting a Band-Aid on a broken arm. To me, the real purpose of a self-talk is for you to figure out what went wrong in your game and why.

In order to have a meaningful self-talk after the game, you need to be "talking" to yourself throughout the game. This is meant to be a quiet conversation, of course. And the essence of the conversation is to focus on how you're going to navigate any unexpected road-blocks, obstacles, and momentary setbacks in your game.

Let me explain.

Think for a moment how many times you have heard a top athlete say in a halftime or postgame interview that "I had to make some adjustments in my game tonight, and fortunately they worked."

*Adjustments* in many ways are the essential difference between a good athlete and a superior one. Why? Because the best athletes know that in order to reach and maintain a level of consistency in their game, they need to become totally objective and scientific about what's off in their game.

This is a key component of becoming a top performer. Good (but not great) athletes tend to be delighted when they have a big game, but in truth, they are hard-pressed to know how to replicate that performance in the games that follow. As a result, their performances tend to be erratic, up and down, with no real rhythm to them.

By contrast, professional athletes know that in order to maintain their high level of performance, that kind of consistency demands more than just being in great physical shape or having practiced one's skills endlessly. It's during the actual games themselves when they are competing when they have to start figuring how to make slight corrections to their game in order to remain steady and to perform well.

Have you ever seen a close-up of an athlete's face in a baseball game, or tennis match, or golf tournament and they seem to be talking to themselves? This is the process of real "self-talks" where the athlete is having a quiet conversation with themselves. And the essence of their self-talk conversation is to focus on how they're going to navigate any unexpected roadblocks, obstacles, and momentary setbacks in their game.

Those slight corrections—mental adjustments—are the true lubricant that allows pro athletes to succeed. Every top performer knows that on any given day, even though they are physically ready to play at their best, there are going to be little imperfections or unexpected shifts that they are going to have cope with.

An example is a basketball player who is efficiently deadly with his jump shot. When he gets to the court, he might find that he's too strong with his shot early in the game, which causes his shot attempts to hit the back of the rim. Mentally, he has to then ever so slightly adjust and calibrate his shooting touch to take a little off his shot so that he can connect.

That's the kind of adjustment I'm talking about. Of course, that's a simple example, but this is what is going on in every player's head during the flow of a game.

Chances are he's not simply telling himself to "buck up" and to "try harder" and "do better." Rather, he's having a deep conversation with himself on how he needs to make a slight, but important, adjustment in his game. That's what the best athletes do.

For example, some years ago, I played in the minors against a terrific hitter named Mike Hargrove. A lefty hitter, Mike made the remarkable jump from Class A ball all the way to the big leagues the following season with the Texas Rangers.

But between every pitch, Mike would call timeout, step out of the batter's box, and seemingly go through a sixty-second routine of all different kinds of actions and motions with his bat, tugging on his batting gloves, adjusting his helmet, and so on. After a while, because of these lengthy actions, he picked up the nickname of "The Human Rain Delay" because it appeared that Mike was either very slow at getting ready for each pitch, or he somehow had to go through all sorts of bizarre superstitious rituals in order to be able to hit.

But it must have worked because Mike had a wonderful career, batting over .300 six times in 12 big-league seasons.

Some years later, I recall talking with Mike when he was managing the Cleveland Indians, and he told me that his between-pitch rituals were just a ruse in order to give him time to think and to reflect a bit on the previous pitch and how he was going to adjust to be ready for the next pitch. In other words, the "rain delay" stuff had nothing to do with superstitions but had everything to do with giving him a chance to recalibrate his swing and to tinker in the most subtle way with his swing.

Looking back, this approach makes a lot of sense. While it may appear to the fan in the stands that the players on the field are just playing their game with no changes, the truth is far different. Every athlete is not only competing against the other players, but also measuring how to make their game more perfect that day. And as Hargrove showed, he made every pitch during each at-bat a real journey as to how he would correct his swing to match the pitching.

That's the essence of making adjustments.

And if you aren't doing that yet, chances are you will eventually come to a point early in your career (perhaps high school, or on a travel team, or in college) where if you don't learn how to make these kinds of adjustments, your progress may plateau.

Why? Because all the other athletes you are competing against—and especially the more experienced ones—are already making adjustments in their game in order to defeat you. They're trying just as hard to make their own game more consistent.

Don't ever lose sight of that reality!

It's those athletes who can learn how to pinpoint adjustments and then make them during the game are the ones who will succeed more often than the others.

Let me put this another way:

A higher level of consistency is the direct result of making successful adjustments.

Immature athletes—meaning those athletes who haven't yet learned how to make adjustments—become easily angered and frustrated when their game isn't working for them. Let's say he's a pitcher who has simply been overpowering the opposing hitters for the first three or four innings and he's been humming along with his fastball.

But then in the fifth inning, either because of fatigue settling in, or because his fastball isn't as fast as before, the pitcher finds the batters catching up to him, and they start to bang out hits. Angered and frustrated by this development, the pitcher just decides to throw even harder. But what he doesn't understand is that even though he *thinks* he's throwing harder, his fastball still comes to the plate at the same speed, and the batters continue to feast on him.

Stunned and even more frustrated, the pitcher continues to get hit around the park, and ultimately loses the game. Afterwards, he's asked why he didn't make any adjustments in the later innings. He protests, "Hell, yes I adjusted. I just started to throw with even more max effort, and yet they still hit me." He then adds to protect his wounded ego, "I think they may have picked up the catcher's signs ... those guys must have known what was coming."

Of course, just throwing harder is not an adjustment. What this young hurler needs to figure out is that as your arm becomes tired during the course of a game, that's when you need to start mixing in some changeups and curves and other off-speed stuff in order to preserve your strength. Every veteran pitcher knows this, and yet, it's remarkable that so few young pitchers understand this. It takes a few games like this before they usually begin to figure it out for themselves. And they discover that as they do begin to change speeds, it makes their fastball appear to be even faster than it really is.

In the parlance of baseball, the kid with the talented arm who just throws hard is just a *thrower*. But the kid who learns how to mix up his pitches and changes speeds is seen as a *pitcher*.

Jeff Passan, the author of the best-selling book, *The Arm: Inside the Billion-Dollar Mystery of the Most Valuable Commodity in Sports*, once told me on my sports radio show, "The vast majority of kids who can throw hard simply do that rather than learn how to pitch because learning how to pitch (e.g., making adjustments) is just too difficult. It's much easier just to go out and rear back and throw at max speed."

In other words, that's just throwing. It's not pitching. There's no sense of adjustments being made.

The very best professional athletes are consistent in their game. And that's where you want to be.

To become consistent, you need to develop the mental agility to make adjustments.

It's not just a matter of endless physical practice and having God-given talent, it's about having and developing the instinctive mental ability to "see" yourself during the game and then having the courage to make small adjustments to keep your game on track.

- Hang a curveball? You need to know immediately to release the pitch a tad later and with a little more snap on your wrist.

- Hit a weak flare to the opposite field? You need to know immediately that you dropped your back shoulder on that pitch instead of waiting longer and hitting down on the ball.

- Your corner kick in a soccer match is too flat and too low to the ground to present any scoring opportunities for your teammates in front of the goal. You need to remind yourself to get a little more loft in your kick by striking the ball a little lower next time.

- You fired a bullet to your wide receiver but it banged off his pads? Make sure you take a little strength off your next pass so that the receiver has a chance to catch it. That's a crucial adjustment that you can and need to make.

With these simple illustrations, you get the idea. And this "internal conversation" needs to go on in every athlete's mind *throughout the game.* And if you aren't having this conversation—this "self-talk" with yourself, then you might find yourself becoming frustrated that your game is not reaching a level of consistency you desire.

I recall playing in plenty of ballgames where I would be mentally exhausted by the time the game ended. Before every pitch, as a second baseman, I would ask myself: "Am I playing in the right spot for this batter? Does he run well—and if so, should I cheat in and play a few steps closer? What is the sun doing in case he hits a pop-up? What about the wind as a factor? What about the infield itself? Is the dirt hard-packed, which will cause a ground ball to scoot faster? Is the grass wet? That will have an impact as well. With a man on first base and a possible double-play ball, can I get to second base in enough time to catch the ball and make a pivot to first?

These and countless other issues of constant adjustment were made on each pitch. It's the nature of highly competitive sports. Of course, all that the fan in the stands sees is a routine three-hopper to the second baseman for an easy putout at first. But trust me, what may seem routine is comprised of all sorts of adjustments being made so that in the end, the play looks simple.

Learning how to make adjustments, and then implementing them, does take a little bit of courage as well as a sense of openness. For example, let's say you're playing a key basketball game, and even though you felt in warm-ups that you were in the zone, when the game actually begins, your first three shots don't connect.

Instead of being off to a fast start with three scores, suddenly that little voice of self-doubt creeps up, and cautions you, *Whoa.... better stop taking shots. You're not helping your team or yourself. Next time you get an open shot, just pass the ball!*

It's during a moment like this that you really need to come up with an adjustment. Ask yourself objectively: *Why are my shots off? Is there a pattern why I'm missing, e.g., are my shots too short? Too strong? Am I rushing them? Not following through properly?*

Whatever the reason is, the sooner you can pinpoint the problem, the better off you will be.

And then comes the hard part. You need to shoot again.

If you miss three shots in a row, it's going to take a little adjustment *and* some personal courage to resume shooting again. Why? Because if you miss a fourth shot, now you're going to feel that you're really letting down your team and yourself.

But in your mind, if you have made the appropriate adjustment, then just the opposite is true: you owe it to your teammates and to yourself to keep shooting.

Why? Because chances are that your coach's game plan in order to win is dependent on your ability to score. And if you become timid, or fearful not to shoot anymore, then you have let that little voice in your head defeat you. All that hard physical work and mental preparation goes down the drain.

It's much better to make the adjustment and then have the courage to try shooting again.

## MAKE THE ADJUSTMENT!!

Remember my mentor Harvey Dorfman, and how he approached top professional athletes? When he figuratively held a mirror up to their face, this was what Harvey was trying to accomplish: *get them to start making adjustments to their game!*

Harvey would begin, "I'm not here to make you feel good about yourself, or to feel sorry for you. You have your friends and family for that.

"You're here to see me because you aren't getting the job done, and you had better start figuring out soon what you need to do to fix the problem."

As you might imagine, big-league stars that weren't familiar with Harvey's blunt, in-your-face approach would be stunned and taken aback. But Harvey plowed ahead.

"My job is to hold a mirror up to your face, and to be honest and candid with you," Dorfman would explain, "because apparently no one in your posse, or even yourself, is being honest with you. Everybody is just saying, 'Hey, don't worry, ace, you'll be OK.' Well, my job is to get you to wake up and to do something about it."

When the star athlete would invariably protest and insist that he didn't know how to self-correct, or that everything he had tried hadn't worked, Harvey would double down even more. "Well, I suggest you take a good long look at yourself and get back to work, because getting back on track is *your* responsibility, not mine."

Harvey would simply conclude by saying: "So what are you going to do about it?"

By this point, Harvey usually had the star player's attention because: a) the star player these days is usually surrounded only by well-wishers and family who only tell him how great he is, and b) the star player may have reached a point where he has lost touch with what he has to do to maintain or find new adjustments in his game.

Dorfman, who was loud, profane, and had a gruff voice, immediately got the attention of these top athletes. I was always impressed with Harvey's ability to take on these superstars in such a blunt and forceful way.

"Rick," Harvey would tell me, "if you're wishy-washy or intimidated by these multi-millionaires, you're not going to be able to help them. They need someone to tell them the truth. And they're not going to hear the truth from their friends, family, agents, or coaches."

But of all the smarts and insights that Harvey provided in his career, perhaps the most important aspect was holding that mythological mirror up to the faces of big-league stars. Getting super-talented athletes to be held accountable for their failures, their foibles, and their lack of making adjustments was perhaps the greatest breakthrough Harvey provided to these stars.

And the sooner you learn how to make your adjustments in a game—and just as importantly, to trust them—the better off and more consistent your game will become.

7

# "WHEN YOU THINK ... YOU STINK"

## THROWING WITH ACCURACY ISSUES

One of the more puzzling situations in sports occurs when—seemingly overnight—either an infielder can no longer throw accurately over to first base, or a catcher can no longer throw the ball back to the pitcher when there are men on base, or for that matter, a pitcher who has excellent control can suddenly no longer find the strike zone.

I'm sure, as a sports fan, you have heard, read, or even seen video of such notable players as Steve Sax, Chuck Knoblauch, Steve Blass, Mark Wohlers, Mackey Sasser, and many others who have been afflicted with this unusual predicament. For years, during their major-league careers, they were excellent fielders, catchers, or pitchers with fine arm strength and no issues with accuracy. But then one day, like being cursed overnight, they no longer can execute good, solid throws.

It's one of the oddest phenomena in all of sports.

I should also point out that this problem is not a new one. It's been around for a while. Clint Courtney, a big-league catcher for several years in the 1950s once confessed to my Dad, who broadcast the original Washington Senators during that era, that he was deathly afraid of throwing the ball over the head of the pitcher when there were opposing runners on third or second base. It was a real concern for Clint. Hal Woodeshick, a Senators pitcher, had immense difficulties in fielding bunts and throwing them accurately to first base. Even though Woodeshick had no problem throwing strikes to the plate, any time he had to field a bunt and throw to first, he had little idea where the ball would land when he heaved it.

And of course, much more recently, look at the mental struggles that Chicago Cubs ace Jon Lester suffers in trying to throw to first base to keep runners tight. As was evidenced especially in the 2016 major-league playoffs and World Series, opposing baserunners would take massive leads off first, knowing that Lester—for some unknown reason—would simply not try to pick them off.

Longtime major-league catcher Jarrod Saltalamacchia, when afflicted with issues in throwing the ball back to the pitcher, apparently developed a method of "tapping" his fingers in an attempt to transfer any anxieties or worries about making a throw into another part of his body. It may sound a little unusual, to be sure, but when an athlete falls into this kind of psychological chasm, finding any kind of solution becomes a top priority.

What many people may not know is that these mental concerns about making seemingly simple throws are not only somewhat routine in baseball, but they have been around the game for years. In fact, I will also confide that in my years working with the Cleveland Indians there were several players who I worked with who also had throwing fears, but they never wanted to go public about it in the worry that it would derail their career. In other words, this issue of throwing with accuracy is a lot more common than many baseball people or fans really know.

Is there a surefire cure for this bizarre malady? In short, no, I'm not aware of any particular form of therapy or approach that can fix this problem quickly. In all the years I've been involved in the field of sports psychology, I haven't met or read any accounts of how a coach or psychologist has "cured" this ailment fully or quickly. Sadly, it continues to be a baffling problem.

That being said, there are those players who do confront the problem, and work tirelessly to make what was once an unconscious and reflexive action—throwing a ball—back into being an unconscious and reflexive action again.

When I work with individual athletes on this issue, I do have my own theory on what causes it, and more importantly, how to overcome it. Perhaps by sharing those insights, this will help some to form a better understanding of the problem.

In June 2000, a reporter named Erica Goode from the *New York Times* did a major feature story about the throwing travails of Chuck Knoblauch, then the second baseman of the Yankees. Among the experts she quoted, Erica asked me for my thoughts. Here's what I said, and this ran on page one of the *Times* that day:

> *Just imagine, suggested Rick Wolff, who worked with the Cleveland Indians from 1989 to 1994 and now is in private practice in Westchester County (NY), consciously analyzing how to place your legs each time you do down a flight of stairs. "Ballplayers, by the time they get to the major leagues know how to automatically run from home to first; they know how to throw a ball," Wolff said. "They don't think about that stuff. But when you start thinking about things, when you start thinking, 'How much pressure should I put into my throw? Should I try to grip the ball a certain way?' you're gone."*

The reporter pressed me as to what might cause such a malady, that perhaps it was caused by outside stress in the athlete's life that might be the source. I said, "There's no rhyme or reason to this. We all have stress in our lives, and major leaguers have stress. I've seen guys who have no cares in the world and they say, 'Rick, I just can't make this play.'" (*New York Times*, June 17, 2000.)

In other words, in my experience, there's no obvious or clear correlation between outside stresses in one's life and then seeing those stresses somehow pop up in one's sudden lack of ability to throw a ball accurately. If anything, most athletes regard going to a ballpark or to a football stadium or to a basketball arena as a kind of personal sanctuary where they can escape all the stresses that may be part of their everyday lives.

That explanation that ran in the *New York Times* about throwing is a very short overview. Let me go into a little more depth.

## WALKING DOWN A FLIGHT OF STAIRS

Let's go back to walking down that flight of stairs. As an athlete, if I were to ask you to walk down a bunch of of steps, chances are you could do that pretty easily and without giving it much thought.

But now, let me ask you this: When you walk down those stairs, *do you start with your left foot first ... or your right foot?*

The truth is, chances are you have never even thought about this before. *You ... just ... go ... down ... the ... stairs.* But this kind of unusual question will force you to pause for a moment and think about whether you lead with your left ... or your right foot. That brief mental pause has suddenly forced you to spend a conscious moment thinking about which foot you start with. And in the world of reflexive sports, that kind of conscious thinking isn't always good.

Of course, it makes no difference at all which foot goes first down the stairs. There is no right or wrong way to descend. But that simple question of asking you about which foot goes first has now introduced a conscious question in your mind; in other words, I have made you begin to think about right or left foot first. And when you pause and think about an action that has always been totally subconscious and automatic, well, the next time you come to a stairwell, I'll bet that you begin to think a bit about which foot to lead with.

And that's all because I asked you a simple question about which foot you lead with when walking down a flight of stairs.

Now, working from that premise, let's carry that over to throwing the ball from second base over to first base in a game. Or, returning a pitch back to the pitcher if you're a catcher.

For years and years as an infielder, whenever you have fielded a ground ball, you have instinctively and routinely thrown the ball to first base. You don't even think about it—you just do it. The action, the motion, the speed, and the direction all come to you *with no conscious thought*.

But suppose one day you do start to think about that throw. You begin to ask yourself about your actions, your motion, the throw's speed, and direction. Like trying to figure how to walk down a flight of stairs, you have accidentally introduced a conscious thought into an action that you have always done forever with no thought whatsoever. You have always instinctively trusted your body and arm to make the throw. But now, you are *consciously* questioning how you do it.

And in short, that's not good.

Here's something else. Have you ever noticed that those infielders or catchers who are afflicted with this issue seemingly lose their fears when they are forced to make an extremely quick or urgent "bang-bang" play? When time is of the essence and the fielder has to make an immediately strong and accurate throw, usually he does so—regardless of the fact that he has extreme difficulty making a routine throw on a routine play when time is not a key.

But once a sense of extreme urgency is at hand, e.g., a throw to first from deep in the hole on a fast runner, or a relay throw from the outfield to nail a runner heading for home, then the infielder makes these urgent throws without hesitation or any inherent worry.

*They have to make this throw now, and make it count.*

That's when one's instincts take over, and any conscious thoughts/worries/anxieties are suddenly pushed off to the side. There isn't time for the fielder to worry about his throw—he just has to make the throw *now*.

Let me present this in another way. For many top and professional athletes, what they do when they compete is so ingrained into their body and mind that when you ask them to explain, they really aren't good at articulating what they did on the field or how they did it. In their book, *This Is Your Brain on Sports*, L. Jon Wertheim and Sam Sommers refer to this as the curse of expertise.

They quote track star Gwen Torrence to explain her inner strategy when she ran and won a race, and Torrence said: "I don't know; the gun goes off and I run as fast as I can, just like I've been doing for as long as I can remember." As the authors point out, she most likely wasn't being coy—she was just being totally honest in not being able to explain her victory.

It's comparable to asking Michael Jordan how he was able to jump so high, or how Willie Mays could run down a long fly ball.

In other words, to paraphrase Nike, they just did it. No inner thought was really needed.

But I would also venture to say that if you started to probe top performers and asked them to really think about how they did these magical things, you might accidentally put them in a place where, by trying to analyze their physical skills too deeply, the could inadvertently sabotage themselves.

Why? Because, sometimes, when you devote too much energy to this kind of mental probing, you end up cutting back on your efficiency—like not being able to throw a ball back to the pitcher.

Often times, athletes, in an attempt to go out and play a totally perfect game, will inadvertently apply too much pressure to themselves. They'll focus, concentrate, and try to almost "will" their way to total success. While pregame preparation is important, some athletes (especially those in high school and college) will think through their game *so* much that they end up blocking their basic physical talents from coming through.

This, of course, is not good. You need to trust your physical skills at game time. If you're thinking too much about how you shoot a basketball or how you throw a spiral or how you're going to hit a curveball, your conscious and analytical mind is going to get in the way of, and interfere with, your fundamental athletic skills.

This is where the phrase *"When you think ... you stink"* comes from.

It means that if you overthink your approach and analysis to your performance, you will actually get in the way of playing well. I know this may sound odd, but too much preparation and too much conscious thought will become counterproductive to what you want to achieve.

Let me return for a moment to how this *"think = stink"* mentality can get in the way of ballplayers who have found themselves in a funk where they can't make accurate or solid throws across a baseball infield.

Let's say you're a second baseman and the batter hits a one-hopper to you. You snag the ball, and because the ball was hit sharply and the batter isn't especially fast, you find that you have an ample amount of time to make a throw to first base.

But that little bit of extra time actually works against you. Why? Because it allows you to *think*.

So, as you take the ball out of your glove, you begin to think about how you're gripping the ball, how it feels in your fingers, to consider where your arm angle should be when making the throw, how strong a throw you should make, and all the other countless little mental details you put into throwing a ball accurately.

The problem is, all of these little instantaneous mental thoughts are not going to result in a perfect throw. In fact, chances are now good that you will make a lousy throw.

How can that be? Because you thought about it too much. Instead of just taking the ball and trusting your instincts, you have tried to mentally design and engineer every part of the throw.

And here's the irony—if the ball had been hit your way fairly slowly, and the hitter runs extremely well, you would have to hurry all of your actions, try to make the play cleanly and then fire the ball over to the first baseman with a solid throw.

Why? Because the nature of this particular play doesn't allow you to have a moment or two to think about what kind of throw to make. *You just had to react.* There was no time to think. You just relied on your pure athletic skills. And it worked.

I can tell you from my work with ballplayers over the years that these two extremes often illustrate the "think = stink" phenomenon. With no time to ponder one's actions, you just do it, and do it well. But with the extra luxury of time to think, that's when problems can crop up.

## THE CURIOUS CASE OF THE QUARTERBACK WHO COULDN'T THROW ACCURATE PASSES

In the August 31, 2015, issue of *Sports Illustrated*, longtime writer Albert Chen did a marvelous feature about the mysterious travails of then–University of Wisconsin quarterback Joel Stave. By all accounts, this was a kid who had the world in the palm of his hand: academically brilliant, handsome, 6-foot-5 and 220 pounds, and athletically gifted. He was being viewed to not only be a star in the Big Ten, but perhaps go on to a career in the NFL.

But then something odd happened to Stave (pronounced STAH-vay).

A couple of weeks before the first game of his junior year (as a sophomore, Stave had enjoyed a very solid season), the head coach at Wisconsin announced that he was going to start another youngster at quarterback instead of Stave.

Stave was, of course, deeply disappointed but said all the right things, and kept himself prepared and ready to go. And to that end, he was tossing the football with one of his buddies one afternoon.

Except that it was hot that day, and as Stave threw the ball, it would occasionally slip out of his hand and the resultant pass was not good.

Stave didn't give this much thought. But the next day, and the day after that, the problem continued. Suddenly, with no warning, Stave discovered that he couldn't throw any short 10- or 15-yard passes accurately. His throws were either into the ground, way over the head of the receiver, or just not close enough.

Undaunted, Stave felt that he simply had to make some adjustments in his passing. As he told *SI*'s Chen: "I'll be throwing it good, throwing it good and then all of a sudden I feel like I hang on to it too long. One will sail, one will slip and then you start thinking, 'Oh, I've got to hang on to it longer.' That's what happens when you start to think too much."

Continues Stave: "then you start trying too hard, trying to force it too much, and you get even more lost."

These kinds of words—and reaction—are commonplace to those who have suffered unexpected psychological roadblocks. And as noted, this kind of thing is very, very common. Perhaps the best known is that of former star Pittsburgh Pirates pitcher Steve Blass who, suddenly, at the top of his game in the 1970s, suddenly lost his ability to throw strikes. Unfortunately, Blass was never able to regain his original form and his career came to an end.

And of course there have many, many others, such as golfer Johnny Miller who struggled with his putting game or tennis star Ana Ivanovic, who inexplicably lost her touch with her service toss. But these are just the well-known athletes; there are lots of others who never wanted to reveal their issues in the fear that it would put a black mark next to their name, and ultimately would end their careers prematurely.

Michael Lardon, a sports psychologist based in San Diego, was quoted in the *SI* article theorizing that Stave had been hit with a kind of a panic attack, perhaps triggered by the upsetting announcement that he was not going to be the starting quarterback for Wisconsin that season. Along those lines, Stave's deep disappointment was now manifesting itself in his seemingly lost ability to throw a football accurately. Such anxiety from losing his starting job may have led to "overthinking and creating an impediment in the reflex loop . . . you get into trouble when you want to be more accurate or perform better. By doing that, [you're] thinking about something that's more reflexive rather than just doing it."

I certainly agree with Lardon that Stave might have decided to "try even harder" to throw better and more accurately, but in the process of attempting to do this, instead of trusting his basic and well-trained reflexive athletic instincts, he short-circuited his talents merely by thinking too much about how he was going to improve his game. (Remember the earlier discussion in this book about "trying easy"?)

It would have been interesting to see what might have happened if Stave had never been relegated to second string. If he had been named as the starting quarterback right from the start, would he have suffered any of these throwing issues? After all, the origin of his throwing problems seems to have been triggered by his sudden demotion. If he hadn't gone through those anxiety moments, can we assume that he would have been fine?

Obviously, we'll never know. But what is interesting is that Stave finally did find a way out of his torment. As part of the solution, he finally acknowledged that he was being too tough, too demanding of himself: "No one's harder on me than myself," said Stave. "Football has always been so important to me. But to get through this, I think it was really about caring less."

An interesting choice of words: caring less. That suggests that he needed to simply go back and rely on his athletic reflexive skills. In any event, Joel Stave got himself back on track, slowly learning to trust himself and his basic athletic instincts again when throwing shorter passes. He went onto have a very productive and solid career at Wisconsin, where he finished with the school record for most wins as a starting quarterback..

# SO, HOW DO YOU SOLVE ALL OF THIS?

How do you block or eliminate these unwanted thoughts and fears from getting in the way of your success? How do you learn to trust your abilities without allowing your fears and self-doubt to get in the way?

Let me try this approach. If I were to stick a pin in your backside when you weren't expecting it, you would immediately jump away in pain. That, of course, is an instinctive and reflexive action. You certainly wouldn't go through the process of first saying to yourself: "That's curious ... I'm experiencing a sharp and painful sensation in my right buttock. I believe that in order to reduce that sharp pain, I should move forward quickly in order to alleviate that negative sensation."

Of course, that's a silly mental process. But I present it to show you how a reliance on conscious thought processes can truly slow down your body's reaction time. Your body was being jabbed by a pin, so it took over and immediately jumped away! There was no need for you to think about it, or to reflect upon a proper course of action. You just jumped away!

That's the same kind of approach you want to have when competing. Don't allow yourself to "think" too much. In other words, you have to learn to trust your body's athletic instincts—because in highly competitive sports, the vast majority of your actions in a game situation are going to be just that: instinctive reactions. *You have to learn to trust your body and yourself.*

There comes a point where you have to trust your body to do the right thing. Trust all of the hours, weeks, months, and years of practice. Your body has been trained to perform in a certain way. Now the time has come to trust it in the same way you know how to run at full speed, or how to stop and shoot a jumper, or how to avoid being tackled in the open field.

You don't think about any of these actions. You just trust your body and your years of athletic experience and competition to make it happen.

I want to make it clear that my approach is simply my own theory; my insights are based upon anecdote and observation. I am not aware of any psychological studies that have definitively come up with a solution. That being said, I still feel strongly that when you spend years and years of your life doing and executing skills via a nonconscious thought, automatic approach, things can often start to go sideways when you begin to start to think, dissect, and analyze your actions.

So how does one break this antagonizing cycle of too much thought?

This is a difficult process, because you have to "train" your mind to eliminate your focusing on the act of throwing. To do that, my experience with athletes has been to try and get them to recalibrate their brains by focusing on the instinctive act of action. Start by making the throw quick and immediate.

Remember when I said that even the most afflicted infielder will make a good, solid, and accurate throw when it's clear that he needs to throw quickly because the play is going to be close? They are able to do that because the urgency of the play doesn't allow them to think and momentarily reflect on how to throw the ball. *They just have to throw it now. They don't have time to stand there and reflect.*

In effect, they haven't got time to think about all of the mechanics or worry about whether it will be a good throw. They just do it. And most times, it's a perfect throw.

Now, when I work with infielders or catchers, I try and take the same approach. I try to get them to actively eliminate the thinking part and convince them that every throw they make over to first base or back to the pitcher has to be done quickly and urgently. As you might imagine, this takes lots of practice over several days in a pregame workout.

The first few rounds of ground balls or receiving pitches should feature immediate throw backs, as though each throw is absolutely urgent. Do that for four sets of a dozen reps each, until the individual begins to become comfortable with throwing the ball without much forethought or worry. Just get him in the rhythm of throwing immediately; don't allow him any time to think and reflect.

Often the athlete will ask, "Should I be focusing on a precise target? Or what should I be thinking about?" I tell them if they really need a target to focus on, they can make it the lettering on their pitcher's or first baseman's chest. But it's not really necessary. And as for what they should be thinking, I often counsel them that it's better not to think about anything.

Why? Because when they were performing well in the past, they didn't think about making their throws at all. They just did them based upon instinctive athletic skill—and that's what we want them to return to.

The next day, repeat the same drill with the same specs. And on the third day and even the fourth day, continue to do the same drills, but as they master these snap throws on a daily basis, gradually tell the individual to pause for a split second before making the throw. They should be able to do this; if not, return to the previous drills and keep doing the reps until they can still make a good throw after a very slight pause. And by the way, remind them to throw the ball hard. Just let 'er it rip!

Once they have mastered that step, make the pause a bit longer on subsequent practice days. You get the idea. You want them to gradually stretch out their pauses, knowing that they have full faith in making clean and solid and accurate throws again because they don't have to think about what might go wrong.

This recalibration, as I call it, does take time. And there might be an occasional setback. But in my clinical work over the years, I have found that athletes feel so relieved that there's a way to find a way out of the woods on this unique dilemma that, psychologically, they feel uplifted and can even relax a bit. Once they see real progress being made, they relax even more. And with relaxation, that self-made hurdle of worrying about bad throws begins to recede.

Now, this is just a general overview. Every player I have ever worked with on these throwing issues had his own unique set of concerns or questions. That's to be expected. But the keys here are to be reassuring, and to practice these quick snap throws so much that, regardless of what the ballplayer might be trying to think about, the throws just become repetitive and automatic. That's the game plan.

And why are the pauses being built in? Because in order to better prepare for real, game-day situations, there are going to be plays in which there are pauses. If he has finally regained trust in throwing via his instincts, then a momentary pause or two is not going to disrupt his ability to make the play and to throw and release the ball accurately.

## OVERCOMING THROWING ISSUES

**DAY ONE:** Have the infield or catcher get into position and upon receiving the ball, have them make an immediate and strong throw to the intended target.

Do not allow them to stop or to reflect. Just make each throw quickly, hard, and accurate.

Do four sets of a dozen throws each.

**DAY TWO:** Repeat the same drill as yesterday. Quick, strong throws. Again, the idea here is to allow the ballplayer to regain a sense of trust about his throwing. If he has difficulty, or makes poor throws, start over.

**DAYS THREE AND FOUR:** Repeat the same procedures, but as he begins to show more signs of relying upon pure athletic instinct, add a momentary pause before he throws the ball—just a quick second to start.

Then instruct him to throw the ball to the target with force and direction. Have this become part of the four sets.

**FOLLOWING DAYS:** This exercise should be continued with gradually longer pauses being built in.

You want the player to become accustomed again to not even thinking about the throw. You just want him to rely upon his basic athletic instinct.

Over time, the goal is that if the fielder/catcher can regain his sense of throwing automatically without thinking about it, then he'll get back into that original comfortable groove that he felt for years. The more he practices making quick throws, the more chance he will come around to defeating and conquering his throwing concerns.

## DEALING WITH THE YIPS IN GOLF

A lot of the conscious thought which gets in the way of throwing a baseball also applies to golfers who suffer unexpected anxiety when putting, even though they had always been successful at putting. And the irony is that, suddenly out of nowhere, they seem to be gripped with an inexplicable sense that they have lost their feel for how much push or strength they should put into their short putts.

In most cases, the golfer will tell you that they never had this problem on the green in years past, and in fact, in some cases, their short game used to be the best part of their game. They looked forward to always having just the right touch to knock the ball into the hole. They made their putts practically on pure instinct, simply relying on their athletic skill.

To me, there are real psychological parallels between golfers who seemingly lose their confidence on the green and ballplayers that suddenly lose their feel in throwing the ball over to first base or back to the pitcher from behind the plate. And the cure with putting is also somewhat parallel.

Have the golfer go out on a practice green, line up dozens of balls all over the green, and then, upon your instruction, have them go out and immediately start to try and putt the balls into the hole. Tell them to go from each ball to the next, as quickly as possible, as though they are up against the clock. Don't worry about trying to line each shot up. Just go over, set one's feet, and aim and fire.

In other words, I just want him to try and regain their athletic touch by not allowing them any extra time so that conscious thought can creep into their physical swing. Just let 'er rip. Tell him to just trust himself.

Again, repetition is always the key here. We're trying to establish a sense of athletic comfort, a zone of success where there is no room for the introduction of conscious thought.

Another case in point: If you talk to any basketball player who is a successful free-throw shooter, there's a pretty good chance that their process of shooting the ball 15 feet into the hoop has become totally absorbed and programmed into their head and body. They are probably so grounded that if you blindfold them, and ask them to shoot free throws by just relying on their athletic instincts, they will surprise you at how accurate they are.

How do they do it? They rely upon their athletic instincts—and not thinking about their process.

OK, back to golf. After several sessions of hitting putts quickly from all over the green where the golfer has become more comfortable at regaining a trust of their athletic ability, then introduce the idea of a few moments of pause and reflection to the golfer. Allow them to approach the putt, think about it for a moment or two, and then when they finally decide to strike the ball, they should just allow their instincts to take over. Eliminate the conscious thought altogether.

It will take several more sessions to convince the golfer to once again trust his own God-given athletic talents. But it does work. And it does take real effort to convince oneself, deep down, to forgo one's inner anxieties about flubbing the putt. But it has to be done in order to move forward.

Some athletes have even developed their own unique internal method of distracting themselves from conscious thought getting in the way of their putting or throwing. When they set up for the putt or for making a throw, they have a default vision in their conscious mind that will actively distract them from the physical task at hand. That vision could be a mental image of anything: a famous picture, or perhaps their girlfriend, their new car, their dog, or whatever. But it needs to be a sharp and striking image of something in their life that is so strong that it consciously distracts them from worrying about throwing or striking the ball.

Why would this momentary conscious distraction work? Because if the athlete is suddenly focused on a different image or concept in their mind's eye, they are not going to be focused on doing a conscious reflection of the putt or the throw. That action is now just left to their athletic instincts to take over. And that's good.

# 8

# ACCOUNTABILITY AND "SELF-TALKS"

You just had a bad game. Nothing went right. Even worse, you knew things were going badly for you, and despite your best efforts to make adjustments in the game, nothing worked.

Bottom line? It was a game worth forgetting.

But on a deeper and more emotional level, the poor performance had the impact of eating away and eroding your sense of self-confidence. Questions start to run through your mind throughout your quiet moments, and often during the course of your sleep, waking you up.

Like unwanted gremlins, these irritating and self-defeating thoughts pop up:

*Maybe I have been fooling myself—perhaps I'm really not as good as I thought I was...*

*Maybe I just can't play at this level...*

*I wonder if the coach has lost faith in me?*

*I wonder how my teammates view me?*

*How will this bad performance affect my playing time?*

*What can I do, if anything, to improve my game immediately?*

If you're a competitive athlete, there's no question that you have most likely suffered a sleepless night or two when you have a game in which things haven't gone your way. It's a most isolating and frustrating feeling.

And yet, while the closest people in your family and circle of friends will tell you, "just brush it off" or, "Hey, everybody is entitled to a bad game every so often," the reality is that you're hurting and devastated, and not really sure how to cope with this.

Questions boil down to: "Was it just one bad game ... or maybe I'm not as good as I thought I was?"

Some sports psychologists suggest that in such times of mental anxiety, you need to have a ready-made kind of "self-talk" that you can build upon in order to regain your mental equilibrium. I guess for some athletes that kind of internal pep talk works, but for the athletes who I have worked with, they seem to respond much more to developing a unique and highly personalized self-talk that is not so much designed to make you feel good, but rather allows you to detail—objectively and without emotion—what you did right and what you did wrong in the game.

In other words, the only way you will be able to learn and to make significant and meaningful adjustments in your game is if you have a self-talk that focuses on what needs to be improved upon.

## DEVELOPING YOUR SELF-TALK

Let me give you an example.

You're a shortstop. Good hands and a strong arm. Excellent speed on the basepaths. Pretty good singles/doubles hitter. A solid fielder.

But in yesterday's game, in a key inning with the score tied and the bases loaded, an opposing batter hit what seemed like a routine double-play ball to you at short. In your haste to make a clean play and make a solid toss to the second baseman to make a pivot—after all, you knew the batter had pretty good speed—you rushed too quickly and momentarily took your eye off the ground ball. Unfortunately, the ball went through your legs for a crucial error as two runs scored.

No one felt worse than you did. You knew that deep down, you should have made that play. Even worse, you had practiced it a thousand times before, and it had become routine for you. The only difference was that that was during practice ... this error had occurred in a real game.

But the damage was done. And the game continued.

In fact, in the bottom of that inning, you came to bat with men on second and third and two outs. Determined to make up for your error in the field, you focused all of your strength into hitting the ball as hard as possible. Indeed, on the first two pitches, you were ready for the pitcher's best fastball. And you were on them; you smashed two line drives that were just foul. Frustrated, sure, but at least you know the pitcher can't get one past you.

Unfortunately, as the pitcher rubbed up a new ball on the mound, he could sense that you were still itching to hit one right on the screws. And to the pitcher's credit, with two strikes, he offered his next pitch right down the middle. But it was a changeup. And it fooled you badly. You took a strong swing, but you were much too ahead of the pitch. You struck out.

Deep, double frustration sunk in. The botched double play and now you strike out with the tying runs on base. Even worse, as you headed back to the dugout, you could see out of the corner of your eye that the manager looked disgusted by your performance, your teammates collectively looked downward, and you noted that the younger infielder who is behind you on the depth chart just got off the bench and is clearly eager to let the manager know that he's ready to take your spot.

Ugh. All bad thoughts.

A terrible day at the ballpark.

You finish the game quietly. You shower and go home.

OK ... so what kind of self-talk do you have with yourself?

Do you berate yourself for playing so poorly? Do you beat yourself up for making that error at shortstop, or for striking out?

Or do you take an opposite tact, giving yourself a private pep talk to recall how good you were in previous games to try and relive some of those earlier games when you had a great performance?

Do you bring out the scrapbook and re-read some of the clippings of those games in which you made headlines? Do you call home just to hear a friendly voice from Mom and Dad? Or maybe call your girlfriend for her support and some words of comfort?

Well, of course, you could do any of these things. And these could all provide a momentary bit of temporary mental salve for you.

But the key word here is *temporary*. Because the reality is, if you don't come to grips with *how* you made those mistakes in the game, and then learn and adapt from those mistakes, then chances are good that you might simply repeat those mistakes again.

In other words, just feeling bad for yourself, or trying to assuage your hurt sense of pride, is not going to change much in your approach to the game.

From my vantage point, an objective self-talk has to be designed in such a way that it's productive and meaningful. It takes some real effort and mental strength to force yourself to somehow step aside from the pain of the plays in the game, and to try and review your actions in an emotionless and scientific manner.

Remember how we talked about visualization *before* the game? Well, this is something in the same vein, except you want to visualize the plays *after* the game. Try to mentally see yourself making that error or striking out (obviously, if there is actual video to be seen, take the time to review that as well).

The point is you need to disassociate yourself from the action in order to better figure out what you did wrong, and how you will prevent that from happening again in the future.

In developing your self-talk strategy after a game, here's the approach I have preached for years to top athletes:

First, it's important to let the bitter emotion of the game and all of your angry adrenaline calm down and subside. You can't do an objective self-talk when the game just finished. Don't even try. Instead, it's OK to let the moment sting in you for a while. That's only natural, and it's to be expected. In other words, if you're a competitive athlete, you are going to feel down about your efforts.

But later, after you have showered and eaten a meal, and have had several hours of quiet time, while the pain is still there, at least it won't be as sharp as it was either during the game or right after. When you reach that quiet-time moment, that's when you need to plan your *inner game analysis*. To do this, it will helpful to have a pen and paper close by, or to write your analysis down on your laptop.

Carefully review from your postgame visualization the error and the strikeout. Replay them in your head, or watch the game video of them. See them in slow motion. Then, be absolutely certain to write down exactly what you felt you did right in those moments (e.g., how you set up for the action, how you moved, etc.). And then more importantly, write down *specifically what you did wrong* in those moments.

- In other words, be sure to pinpoint and analyze what you need to do to keep you from making those mistakes again. Don't get frustrated or upset with yourself. This is just mental postgame adjustment time. Be scientific in your analysis. Rather, shift your direct focus to what you should have done, and more importantly, what you will do to make the key adjustments in the future. For example, with that ground ball that went between your legs, perhaps you write down: *Got into fielding position a little too slowly. Should have been quicker to get down.*
- *Assumed that the ball would take a high hop and it didn't.*
- *Realized the batter was fast, and as such, hurried to make the play quicker than it needed to be.*

- *Need to realize that I have to first field the ball before making any kind of play.*
- *Need to get into position sooner, quicker, and keep my body much lower.*

These are the kinds of simple postgame self-adjustments that an infielder needs to bear in mind. And if you write all this down, you'll be amazed at how much you incorporate and will learn these lessons for the future. The physical act of writing these notes down in your journal or notebook is important. Just like taking notes in class, and preparing for a test in school, writing down the essential points of your performance will stay with you.

Sound simple? My best advice is to try it. The way the human brain works, when you write down important points, your mind-body tends to keep that information in a very secure place ... and best of all, you won't forget it.

This is the kind of self-talk that will actually pay off down the road. Some athletes call it learning from experience or from one's mistakes. Others see it as a kind of reality check. Whatever term you use, it's important your self-talk doesn't focus on just blaming yourself for having a bad game or for letting your teammates down. Nor is it about convincing yourself just how good you are as an athlete. Rather, this is about learning how to make important adjustments from your own individual inner game analysis.

## TURNING A BAD DAY INTO A POSITIVE

The biggest concern, of course, is if you go out and then make the same mistakes again. For example, you continue to get fooled by a changeup with two strikes. You forget to get your body down all the way to field a ground ball. Whatever the mistake or miscue happens to be, without the benefit of an objective review of what you did wrong *and* how you plan to correct it, well, you run a serious risk of continuing to make the same kinds of mistakes. Do that, and your career will come to an end far earlier than you expected.

Why? Because all coaches and scouts, no matter the sport, can truly sympathize and understand that an athlete can have a bad day. Hey, it happens. We're all human and are prone to error. But what the better coaches and scouts look to see is if you continue to make the same mistakes repeatedly without making an adjustment. When you start to get to that point, then they will just assume that you don't have the ability to react to and correct your errors. That's not a good image to have following you around.

So, in my experience, the best way to counteract these in-game mistakes and errors is by taking positive steps to confront them and then correct them by doing a careful analysis of what went wrong, and what you can do to make sure you don't do them again. Writing them down along with your own, self-prescribed approach to fix these problems is a very strong step.

Does this mean that you'll never strike out again, or never make another error fielding a ground ball? Of course not. But what it does mean is that if you ever find yourself in a close game where you need to make an important play in the field, you will be mentally prepared and ready to execute the right play. Or, if you come to bat and find that you're ready to rip into the pitcher's fastball, you will also be mentally prepared to expect a possible changeup.

To me, this is the essence of developing a sense of mental experience. Coaches talk all the time in all sports about "rookie mistakes" or young players not having enough game experience. But when those coaches are asked how young athletes develop that kind of game experience, they simply reply by saying the players need to play a lot of games before that sense of experience sinks in.

I would suggest that a young player can speed up or expedite the process of getting through the hassle of rookie mistakes by implementing this kind of individualized postgame mental analysis of one's performance. Yes, it's a bit like doing homework—just like the kind of homework you had to do when you came home from a game in high school. And just like school homework, this is important for any athlete who wants to take their game to the next level and feel as though they are working hard to improve their overall game.

The bottom line is that most athletes know that they need to spend some time before each game or contest to mentally prepare themselves to focus on the event. Look at the legendary Olympic swimmer Michael Phelps, and no matter how many times he swam competitively, he would always put on a serious game face and hide away from everyone for at least a half an hour before each race so he could concentrate. Countless other athletes do the same thing.

But those athletes who also take the time to focus *after* the game or contest on what they did right, or more importantly, what they did wrong, and how to make a key adjustment to ensure that next time they get it right ... well, those are the athletes who will continue to see their overall game improve steadily over the course of a season.

# 9

# THE POWER OF THE MENTAL CUE CARD

ONE OF THE MOST IMPORTANT techniques I learned from Harvey Dorfman was a written device he called the mental cue card.

In short, the card is just what it sounds like: the athlete writes down four or five very short bullet points on a standard white index card that are truly personalized and unique to helping that athlete stay mentally focused for the upcoming game.

The card might sound simple in concept, but it's actually a very powerful tool. That's because it's designed to be very, very specific to the individual athlete. Indeed, it's the athlete who is charged with the responsibility of putting the card together with its specific mental reminders.

In other words, the card's contents are comprised of those key points that the athletes knows that he or she has to focus and lock on in order to perform well. General reminders like: "Keep a positive approach" or "Always give 100 percent effort" are nice sentiments, but they are not the purpose of this card.

Rather, and especially if the athlete has been struggling with poor performances or has been in a recent slump, the mental cue card highlights what the athlete needs to do to succeed. I recall working with a veteran major-league outfielder who found himself in a batting slump because he was swinging too soon and, as a result, he was pulling outside pitches and they were becoming easy fly outs or weak grounders to short.

Remember, with big-league pitchers routinely throwing at 90-plus mph, hitters have to react so quickly at the plate that, sometimes, especially with right-handed hitters, there's a natural tendency to want to swing too soon at a pitch. When you do that, and you release your swing even a moment too soon, there's a good chance you are going to either be fooled badly by the pitch, or you will hit a routine ground ball to the shortstop or second baseman.

In other words, you won't make good solid contact. Do that over the course of several at-bats, and just like that, you're in a slump.

Major-league hitters need to be absolutely precise for every pitch. As such, this particular hitter studied lots of videotape and worked extensively with the team's hitting coach. But he still wasn't finished. He came to me to help prepare an individualized mental cue card that he could review not only before the game, but also *during the game*. He had his index card placed into a plastic slipcase and he literally kept it in the back pocket of his uniform pants. It became an essential element of his game-day equipment.

His batting preparations listed on his cue card were very specific to him:

| |
|---|
| • Always remember to sit back—wait longer on the pitch |
| • Always be focusing on hitting each pitch to right field |
| • Curves/sliders *cannot* at any time be pulled |
| • Always be absolutely ready to swing at the first pitch |

I must admit I would receive a sense of personal pride whenever I saw this player in the on-deck circle in games, and he would routinely take out his mental cue card and review it. I felt even better when he would then lace a line drive into right-center field for a solid base hit.

## HOW TO WRITE YOUR OWN MENTAL CUE CARD

Any athlete can put together their own mental cue card. But to make it effective, you have to first determine those key elements of your game that you need to focus on in order to perform at a top level. For some athletes, especially the younger ones, this might be difficult to pinpoint. For other athletes, the cue card might be a reminder, as with the major-league outfielder above, of what to bear in mind in order to avoid repeating the common mistakes that might lead to a continued slump.

By the way, mental cue cards can be rewritten and adjusted at any time. If you feel things have shifted in your game, then certainly make those adjustments in your cue card. The beauty of the card is that it's meant to reflect a detailed and in-depth game plan of what you need to do to perform well.

You may have seen athletes improvise with their mental cue cards. For example, they may write a key phrase or reminder in ink under the bill of their baseball cap. Or in some cases, they will write a key mental phrase on their sneakers, or on a wristband they wear during the game, or just write it in ink on the palm of their hand so they can refocus during the course of the game.

So, what's the bottom line? Do mental cue cards work? Well, judging from the success of so many of Dorfman's athletes, and from many I have worked with over the years, I believe that mental cue cards can have a real positive impact for those who use them.

In effect, mental cue cards provide an added cushion of confidence to the athlete. While they have physically prepared and worked hard in practice leading up to the game, and have presumably taken the time to mentally prepare themselves through visualization, they also formalized a quick mental set of guidelines in which they are trying to eliminate outside distractions and are now focused on a solid and consistent approach. These mental cue cards work as a kind of insurance policy to help bolster the athlete's frame of mind when things "speed up" during the game. Referring to this cue card allows them to settle things down a bit, and to recalibrate.

## PUTTING TOGETHER YOUR PREGAME PREPARATION

We've been discussing postgame evaluations and in-game mental cue cards. Let's back up for a moment and review how to prepare for a game.

For most athletes, they usually have developed their own pregame routines by the time they enter high school. Such a routine might involve getting up at a certain time, to have the same kind of breakfast and lunch, to watch a favorite inspirational movie, and of course, to listen to their individual choice of music in the locker room.

This is all good. But I would ask you to take your game day preparation one step further. You should take a moment to think through and analyze your routine and to see if there are parts of your preparation that can be enhanced or improved.

For most of us, we usually just find ourselves doing things that seem comfortable and have become something of a habit. And of course, falling into the same routine or doing the same rituals is part of the superstition programs that many athletes do. My challenge to you is this: perhaps you can better focus your pregame routine to not only streamline it, but to concentrate on what you want to accomplish in the upcoming contest.

Try to map out and outline those specific activities that are going to get you thinking on the right track for the game. For example, look at the theoretical chart below for a professional baseball player who has a night game starting at 7 p.m.

**Morning hours.** Devoted to personal errands, chores, laundry, breakfast, etc. The game still seems far off. You should be aware of it, but at this point of the day, are just doing busy stuff.

**Lunch from 2 p.m. to 3 p.m.** This should be a fairly big meal because you only want to eat light snacks and hydrate as the game approaches. Game time is now beginning to loom in your mind's eye.

**Post-lunch.** Take 20 to 30 minutes to go through your visualization routine while you're resting in a dark and quiet room.

**Arrive at the ballpark at 4 p.m.** When you physically enter into the ballpark, take a brief moment to remind yourself that you are now consciously leaving your personal life, concerns, hassles, and everything else behind.

Once you go into the ballpark, your total focus now needs to be on your upcoming performance, not on whether you paid the electricity bill on time, or about the argument you had with your girlfriend that morning. All those distractions are to be left outside the ballpark.

The good news is that for most athletes, leaving the world's problems and concerns away from the ballpark is always welcome. Most athletes thoroughly enjoy this respite from everyday life. The clubhouse or locker room and field is a soothing and private sanctuary where ballplayers can smile, relax, crack wise comments at each other, and in effect, they can feel good about themselves.

Believe it or not, this jovial camaraderie is an important component when mentally relaxing oneself to compete. Locker rooms where the atmosphere is tight or quiet and where players don't kid around with each other suggest that the athletes are too mentally constipated and suppressing real nervous anxiety. Most coaches and managers are sensitive to this kind of environment and will do what they can to get the players to open up, relax, and joke around.

**Equipment check at 4:15 p.m**. Go through your uniform and equipment needs for tonight's game. Too few athletes take the time to make sure their equipment is ready to go, whether it's checking one's shoes to make sure they're in good shape, or one's baseball bats, fielding gloves, sunglasses, athletic cup, and so on.

This may sound silly, but there's nothing worse than to be in the middle of a game only to discover your shoelaces just snapped, or that your baseball bat has a slight crack in the handle that you hadn't noticed before. The point is, when you're preparing for the game, this is the right time to check on these matters. You don't need this kind of distraction when the game is on.

**Video review at 4:30 p.m**. Spend 15 to 20 minutes going through the videotape of your last performance. Make mental notes of whatever key adjustments you need to make. This will have the effect of locking your thoughts on the challenges for tonight's game.

**Review your mental cue card at 5 p.m**. After the video session, reinforce your key adjustments by going through your mental cue card. Update your card if necessary. Try and keep your adjustments simple and easy to follow.

If you can, keep your mental cue card handy throughout the game so you can always refer to it, if needed. Consider it as a trusted companion that will serve as a true compass for you in terms of maintaining your sense of equilibrium if and when things don't go the right way for you.

**Out onto the field.** When you head out for stretching exercises, batting practice, or extra work, you should now be totally locked in on those elements of your game that you want to focus on that night.

Your mind-set should be one of a balance of confidence along with an undercurrent of easiness and relaxation, as in, *I know what I want to do ... I know I have done it in the past ... and I fully anticipate doing it again tonight.*

# AND NOW, YOUR POSTGAME ROUTINE

Ironically, while so many athletes pay a great deal of attention to their pregame routine in order to sharpen their preparation, very little active attention is paid to their postgame routine.

When the game is over—regardless of whether you won or lost or how you did—you will need at least 15 to 20 minutes to let your emotions calm down. This is why most locker rooms are closed to the media for at least 20 minutes after every game—just so athletes are allowed to chill.

As for you individually, as you get undressed and shower, this is the time to start to review your game and to go through an inner checklist of how you felt you did during the game. But one word of caution—as you review your performance, try to see if you can review your good points and not-so-good points in a professional and objective manner.

Let me explain. Amateur athletes tend to focus on those moments of the game when they did something really special, such as getting a big hit, scoring a touchdown, or making a terrific shot from the corner. Uplifted by that magical moment, amateurs look back and reflect *only* on that key play as the defining moment of their performance that night.

The truth is, they may have struck out three times, or missed several blocks in the backfield, or missed a bunch of easy shots. But for the amateur athlete, all of these not-so-good moments are washed away by their big play.

For the pro athlete, though, this is not an appropriate response. Sure, it's nice to have gotten the big hit. And you should feel very good about that. But then again, that's what you expect yourself to do, that's your job.

But likewise, striking out three times has to be seen in the same balanced light. You can't let yourself get too high or get too low by the extremes in your performance. Rather, the professional looks upon the night's performance as a kind of personal jigsaw puzzle, and should be thinking as they head out of the clubhouse to get some dinner with teammates and friends: *OK, I got the big hit when I made that key adjustment to my batting approach in the ninth inning. But why did it take me three previous at-bats—where I struck out each time—to make that important adjustment to my swing?*

When you start thinking along those analytical, scientific, and non-emotional lines, then you know you are starting to approach your game as a true professional, not as an amateur who just focuses on how exciting it was to get that big hit.

Trust me, that's a huge step forward.

## LEARNING HOW TO BECOME TRULY OBJECTIVE ABOUT YOUR TALENTS

Along the same lines of becoming analytical about your skills is the gradual recognition of what your actual physical talents are.

This too is part of the overall maturation process for all athletes as they rise and develop through their careers. In short, you need to take stock of what you do especially well ... and likewise, which skills are perhaps beyond your reach.

Without this kind of self-evaluation, you might find yourself short-circuiting your career.

Let me give you an example. When I was growing up, I was a fan of the old Washington Senators. They had an infielder who was a slick fielder and a fair hitter (I'd rather not give his name since he was a family friend). And every so often, he would hit a pitch just perfectly and he would send it over the cavernous wall in left field at old Griffith Stadium.

Problem was, whenever this light-hitting infielder would hit a homer, he must have become so elated with his newfound power that he would then try and hit a home run on every subsequent at-bat. As you might imagine, the results were disastrous. Instead of "staying within his abilities," he must have recalled how much fun and heightened self-esteem he must have enjoyed when circling the bases on his over-the-fence shot.

Of course, that home run was much more of a fluke (he only one or two a year) than an indication that he had suddenly discovered more power at the plate. Rather than just recognizing that he was primarily a singles and doubles hitter—which is what got him to the big leagues in the first place—he began to lengthen his swing so that he could aim for the fences. After all, I'm sure he was well aware of the old baseball cliché that "home-run hitters drive fancier cars."

As a result, the more that this fellow tried to hit for power, the more he, in turn, ruined his overall batting average. Instead of hitting line drives in the gaps, he was now popping up, hitting weak grounders, and even worse, striking out with increasing regularity. His batting average would just sink.

In effect—and again, this was in the days before videotape was available, or for that matter, hitting coaches weren't really in vogue—this infielder would find himself deep in a slump, all because he had hit a home run and thought he could now change his approach to hitting. It would take him a couple of weeks before he could straighten himself out, shorten his stroke, and go back to his regular hitting approach. But by then, he would have lost valuable points on his overall batting average.

The point is: as you ascend the ladder in sports, you need to become acutely aware of what precise skills you possess and what you need to do to take advantage of them. More so, you need to know how to rein yourself back in if you happen to overstep the normal boundary lines of your talent level.

That may sound obvious and simple, but the truth is that too many athletes either lose sight of their skill level, or even worse, they start to think that their other skills can be heightened simply by focusing on them for a while.

Here's the reality. As a baseball player, if you have superior running speed on the bases, you need to make that your primary talent. Learn all that you can on how to maximize that skill, either by learning how to bunt for a hit, how to bat left-handed so you're closer to first base, how to slap down on the pitch so you eliminate fly balls and popups, how to take big leads when on base, how to make the pitcher nervous with your presence on the bases, and so on.

But if you simply take your speed for granted, or don't try to maximize its potential, then you are basically wasting a great talent. The same applies to a pitcher who has a terrific curveball or changeup but is reluctant to throw it. If you have these kinds of talents—but don't take advantage of them—your career is not going to develop. Amazingly, you'd be surprised at how many top athletes don't recognize their real skills—the talents that scouts first noticed, and which ultimately got the player signed. For the truly accomplished player, they know by the time they reach the collegiate or professional levels what precise skills they possess that will propel them to the next higher level.

As such, you need to have a hard talk with yourself as to what your top skill or skills really are, and how best to utilize them in order to progress your game. If you're not able to do this, then sit down with your coach and ask him. Don't worry—he'll know exactly what you do well, and what you should keep on doing to get to the next level.

# 10

# "STAY IN THE MOMENT" AND FIND YOUR FOCAL POINT

I'VE LONG BEEN A BIG admirer of Ken Ravizza, the famed sports psychologist who is based primarily on the West Coast. Ken talks all the time about players staying "within the moment." That means that during the course of any competitive game, there are going to be both good and not-so-good moments. When something good happens, well, most athletes have no problem feeling confident about themselves and their efforts.

But when something bad happens, that's when the athlete is challenged. That's when the athlete needs to be able to somehow isolate that poor play and just leave it in the moment ... and then move on.

Easier said than done, for sure. But when things go wrong, you need to fully focus on it for just a few seconds—and then consciously push yourself to move on so you can concentrate on the *next* play which is coming your way.

If you allow yourself to become distracted by a poor play or personal mistake—a play which, for all intents and purposes, has now come and gone—you then run the risk of not being ready for the next play, or for the rest of the game. You need to put that bad moment in the immediate past, and then continue to press ahead and prepare for the next big play.

Says Ken in the April 22, 2016, issue of *Collegiate Baseball*: "As a baseball player, you don't have control of what is going on around you. *You can only control how you choose to respond to it* (italics added). You have to be in control of yourself before you control your performance."

The idea, of course, is to always keep your emotions in check. You know by now that when you allow your emotions to run wild during the course of a competitive game, that can often get in the way of your execution of your athletic skills. Whether you're trying to shoot free throws in a close game, or sink a key three-foot putt, or break a curve over the outside corner, runaway emotions can only get in the way of your goals.

That's when taking a few seconds to collect your mental focus is absolutely essential.

And while Ravizza is addressing his advice primarily to baseball players, the same approach applies to athletes in any sport. If you want to gain control and allow yourself to perform at your top level, first *you need to learn how to control your performance*. Not only will that make you feel more comfortable and confident, but it will have the effect of slowing the game down all around you.

There are several ways in which you can take command of your game and remain focused. But above all, you need some sort of base point that you can mentally refer to in order to get your game on track. For some, this can be some sort of personal mantra, or short phrase, that you know that, deep down, whenever you utter this phrase under your breath it will bring you back to your center point. That center point is that psychological level of stability that you need in order to stay in control of your game and, ideally, get back into the zone.

Sometimes, as mentioned earlier in the book, during a close-up of a pitcher during a televised game, you might see the pitcher appear to be talking to himself in a very quiet or private way. In many cases, this is when the pitcher is simply acting as his own best friend, and is verbally reminding himself how to stay on track and how to get through a difficult inning.

Other athletes will recalibrate themselves by locking in on perhaps a favorite song, or perhaps a visual image of a very special moment in their lives. It doesn't really matter what your base point is—but what does matter is that it allows you to mentally regroup, refocus, and reload in a quick and positive way so you can regain control of your game.

Ken Ravizza talks about athletes having a focal point that they can turn to at any moment in a game where that specific base point instantly allows the individual to regain their mental equilibrium and sense of purpose. Your focal point could be anything in the ballpark, just so long as it remains constant. You could use the flagpole as a focal point to settle yourself down. Or perhaps an advertising sign on the outfield fence. (By the way, Robert Nideffer, another accomplished sports psychologist and the author of *The Inner Athlete*, is another advocate of finding a focal point.)

Whatever you select, you should choose this focal point well before the game begins. Lock it into your head. Tell yourself that, as your focal base point, whenever things seem to be getting out of hand or choppy during the game, or you feel yourself becoming a victim of your emotional ups and downs, that's the time to take a moment and lock hard onto your focal point to get back on course.

Let the moment sink in. The focal point should give your mind a rest in order to reset your approach, your emotional mind-set, and your confidence.

After "refreshing" yourself for a few seconds, you can go back to your task at hand.

# CASE STUDY: ANDY MURRAY LOSES FOCUS IN THE 2016 US OPEN

Here's a classic example of not being in the moment—of allowing one's emotional mind-set to creep up and ruin one's day. This happened to one of tennis's premier players.

Andy Murray, who had been the most consistent player on the ATP Tour all summer, was the gold medal winner in men's singles at the Rio Olympics. He was the number two seed in the US Open. He was very close to being on top of his game.

But against Kei Nishikori in the quarterfinals of the 2016 US Open, Andy's game became unglued. He was actually leading in the match, two sets to one, but then it started to rain at Arthur Ashe Stadium in Flushing, New York. Play was stopped to close the roof and to dry off the court. When play resumed, Murray continued to lead the match. But then, an inexplicable and unexpected gong sound went off during a point, apparently causing Murray to lose his focus. The point was replayed.

But the damage to Murray's concentration was done: he was observed to be upset by these distractions. According to the *New York Times*, he was even bothered by a moth that was flying around on the court. Angered then by a poor shot, Murray smashed his racket on the top of the net out of total and atypical frustration.

His opponent, Kei Nishikori, kept his focus, however, and before too long, he had defeated Murray and it was Nishikori who advanced to the semifinals.

Andy Murray is a seasoned pro. And he's very consistent. But for whatever reason, his mental focus was derailed in the middle of the match, and even though we can assume he made every attempt to "live in the moment" and to move behind the rain delay, and that loud, unexpected noise, the moth, and so on, he clearly couldn't rein in his emotional temperament. And ultimately, it cost him his match.

Murray, of course, has since moved on, and is still one of the world's top tennis players. But the point is, if he can lose his focus and concentration that quickly and easily, it's clear that any competitive athlete can fall prey to the same kind of mental unraveling.

## EMBRACE YOUR NERVOUS ANXIETY—DON'T FIGHT IT

Every athlete knows that competing in sports is a most emotional undertaking. If you aren't psyched up to compete in the game, then you're not really prepared to compete that day.

But here's the irony. If you allow your emotions to get in the way of your performance, you then run the risk of losing control and of not getting the job done.

That's most ironic because all athletes start games with great emotion, and with tremendous amounts of adrenaline running through their bodies. Think about that. When you run out onto the field, or take the court, or skate out onto the ice, or whatever sport you compete in, you know what I'm talking about. Whether it's the pride of being a top competitor, or of wearing the school's uniform, or of just wanting to play well that day, your body at that point is fueled by tremendous emotion.

And yet, to succeed that day, you then have to turn down the gauge on your emotions in order to be able to play at your level. You have to bring it all down and become much more businesslike and, well, professional, in order to get the job done.

You often hear about athletes having the jitters before a game, or having butterflies in their stomach. That's all raw emotion, of course. But then you also hear the athlete say that, "Once the first pitch is thrown or the first play is over, then the butterflies are gone, and I can concentrate on my game."

This is exactly what I'm talking about. You need to suppress the emotional component of your game if you want to succeed on any given day. You can't really stay locked in and focus entirely if you allow your emotions to get in the way.

This is not to suggest that you either need or want to get rid of your nerves either before or during competition. Believe it or not, when your body gives you that shot of adrenaline, or you sense butterflies in your system, don't try to dismiss those feelings.

Why? *Because those feelings are good.* It's your body telling you it's now fully primed and ready for total action. Some sports psychologists tell you to try and get rid of nerves. I'm telling you just the opposite: embrace your nervousness as a welcome sign that you're focused and locked in.

I was reading an article by Bill Pennington of the *New York Times* (July 15, 2016) about pro golfer Bradley Keegan and how he deals with nervous anxiety when he's playing in a major tournament. Said Keegan: "If I feel nervous, I just feel it, try to accept it and move on. I don't try to block it out."

In fact, Keegan has found that going through the process of just trying to block out the nerves is something of a distraction that he doesn't need. Besides, as he adds, "When you feel nerves, it's a good thing. It means you're doing something right."

Just a few years ago, that kind of approach—of looking forward to nervous anxiety—was usually dismissed by sports psychologists. But these days, as Bradley Keegan suggests, nervousness should be regarded as a positive and reassuring sign that you're on your game.

In other words, you have to become much more aware of the balance in your body between your nerves and any other emotions that might get in the way of your game. You can, and should, be a little bit nervous. That prepares and readies your body for competition. And the emotion of nervousness is not to be blocked or shunned.

However—and I acknowledge this is a subtle difference—you have to try and keep other distracting emotions under control. Those emotions—ranging from outbursts of joy to sharp depths of disappointment—can and will have a negative impact on your game.

## PUTTING YOUR EMOTIONS INTO A STONE ... AND THE POWER OF HUMOR

Here are two other methods to help an athlete cope with an in-game stressful situation:

Ken Ravizza, along with his sports psychology colleague Tom Hanson, has also talked about another method of getting rid of one's negative emotions—that of mentally transferring all of your negativity or poor plays into a small stone or rock.

That is—and admittedly this is more symbolic than anything else—taking a moment to quickly review the things that are not going well for you in today's game, and then picking up a small stone. Try to mentally transfer all of those not-so-good feelings from your brain into that inanimate rock and then simply take that stone and toss it far, far away.

Psychologically, of course, the idea of transferring your negative thoughts and experiences into that rock or stone, allows you to give your head a quick and clean and fresh start. No more bad plays! All the negative energy has been crammed into the rock and they are all now out of your head. And now, of course, the stone has been tossed away so they are no longer part of your mind and body.

Does this work? Hey, like all sports psychology tools, it depends on the individual. But it's certainly worth considering if you're in a bad slump.

Here's another way to derail tension when things seem to be ganging up on you in a game. Rick Peterson, the longtime pitching coach, talks about the power of humor to deflate a tight situation. Peterson is a big advocate of letting the pitcher's tension dissipate by simply getting him to laugh or smile for a few seconds.

In Peterson's years of experience, once a player has a lighthearted moment to chuckle at a funny quip or observation, that release allows the pitcher to psychologically get out from the burden of the moment by reframing one's predicament. That allows the pitcher to internally regroup and come back at the problem at hand with greater enthusiasm.

In his book *Crunch Time*, Peterson tells a very funny story about working with All-Star reliever Jason Isringhausen who, caught in a real jam in the ninth inning of a game at Yankee Stadium, was close to becoming unglued on the mound. Peterson hustled out to the mound to see what the problem was with Izzy.

"Rick," Izzy began, "I can't feel my legs."

Peterson listened and smiled gently and said: "That's okay; we don't need you to kick a field goal."

The funny line quickly hits its mark. Izzy roared with laughter... the tension was broken, and he was able to reframe the situation and go back to work with the relief that a single funny line can bring.

I happen to be a big supporter of the power of humor. In all sports, there are always moments of intense focus and pressure. But for those athletes who can respond to a funny quip or maintain a sense of humor about what's going on, I find that those individuals have a much better time in coping with the pressure of the moment.

When I was the head baseball coach at Mercy College and later with the Cleveland Indians, I consciously did my best to conduct conversations during tough times in a game with a smile and, if possible, a funny line. After all, if your athlete picks up on the fact you're just as tight and nervous as they are, that only reinforces their anxiety.

When an athlete is already tight with tension, the last thing they need to hear or see is a coach who is just as nervous as they are, pacing in the dugout and looking like a caged animal. That only ratchets up the nervous anxiety in the athlete. Or even worse, the coach angrily barks orders at the competitor, instructing them to "buck up" or "get it done" or "fight through it."

On the other hand, if you appear calm, relaxed, and can maintain your sense of humor, that's only going to get your athlete to relax and reframe. And that's the ideal situation.

# IF YOU TRY TOO HARD, YOU WILL FAIL

You *always* need to stay within your relaxed range of concentration and physical delivery. Trying too hard will only make you less effective.

That may sound like a paradox, but the truth is, you need to stay within your expectations and within your normal rhythm during times of game stress. For example, if you find yourself gritting your teeth, or psychologically push yourself to redouble your efforts, ironically, that's when the wheels will begin to fall off.

Pushing oneself too hard will only serve to mess with your basic mechanics and rhythm. Pitchers are often very guilty of this. In a tight spot, they will try to "hump up" and throw even harder to get out of a jam. But as Rick Peterson points out in *Crunch Time*, trying too hard will have the result of throwing your mechanics off-kilter, and will actually lead you down the wrong pathway.

In short, his advice is to stay calm and stay within your comfortable frame of reference. Don't give in to the temptation of trying even harder. In short, the results you want will not come. Staying within one's limits is absolutely crucial, especially during critical times in a game.

# WHAT IS SELF-HYPNOSIS?

I chased the concept of self-hypnosis for years when I was actively playing. I mean, how cool would it be if I could somehow train my mind and body to perform at a consistently high level?

But as much as I tried to chase this wonderful idea and pin it down, the more frustrated I became. As far as I could tell, there just wasn't any well-prescribed approach to self-hypnosis, or the process in which you simply put yourself into some sort of psychological trance so that when you "wake up" you will take your body and mind to a higher level of performance.

Again, it all sounded wonderful in theory. But for the life of me—and believe me I tried valiantly—I could never seem to make this work for my own game.

The self-hypnosis books and papers I read suggested that in order to reach your goals, you first had to:

- Relax oneself in a quiet and darkened room
- Close your eyes
- Take deep, gentle breaths
- Concentrate solely on the specific aspects of your game where you wanted to excel
- Develop some sort of personal "trigger" points that you can rely upon that would subconsciously remind you of the proper pathway you want to follow

The problem was, the more I studied this, the more I gradually realized that the process of self-hypnosis seemed to be fairly similar in its approach and development to visualization. And that's OK, because I think that visualization does work and can have a significant impact on an athlete's mental approach to improving their game.

To me, the bottom line is that whether you go with self-hypnosis or with visualization techniques, in the end the overall idea is to align your mind with your body. Most importantly, you want to cut through all the outside clutter, distractions, and emotions so that your brain can better direct your body's voluntary muscles to perform at a consistent level.

## THE MYTH OF CHOKING

Let me just say this: I really dislike the term *choking*, as in a player or a team "choked" in a clutch situation.

Not only is it a most derisive and offensive term, but over the years it's usually used by fans of the game—the spectators up in the stands or those watching television. Of note is that you rarely find professional athletes or coaches using the word, because the term carries with it a devastating blow to the individual, as if the athlete in question wasn't giving their best.

But from the fan's perspective, they don't see that. All they see is:

*How could he miss that easy layup that would have won the game? Talk about a choke artist!*

*All Bill Buckner had to do was handle a routine grounder! He choked in the World Series.*

You know what I'm talking about.

Now, on one hand, nobody expects a player at any level to make an unexpected or brilliant play in the key moment of a game. That's understood. But when a top pro or college athlete is called upon to make a relatively straightforward or routine play—and then somehow muffs it—it's at that point where the fans pile on with unforgiving taunts about that athlete being a choker.

Of course, no athlete ever wants to miss an easy putt, or miss a key free throw, or blow a routine extra-point attempt. I think we can all agree with that. But it *does* happen. And I think we can all agree with that as well.

So there are two questions:

Why does an athlete screw up on such an important but easy play?

And how does an athlete move on when he or she suddenly realizes that they've made a terrible blunder?

Of course there is no universal explanation that covers all late-game mistakes. But my theory is that top athletes are so often focusing and thinking ahead to the next play that they sometimes allow their concentration on the immediate task at hand to be momentarily ignored, almost subconsciously:

*I know this easy layup is a gimme ... but then I gotta immediately hustle back on defense.*

AND HE MISSES THE SHOT!

*Once I sink this gimme for par, I'm really looking forward to crushing my tee shot on the next hole so I can put myself back in the lead.*

### BUT HE RIMS THE CUP!

*I lead off the next inning and I'm starting to think about what I can expect from the pitcher during that at-bat while I handle this routine ground ball.*

### BUT HE DOESN'T GET DOWN AND THE BALL GOES THROUGH HIS LEGS!

For the fans and pundits who observe these heartbreaking errors, very often their sense is that the athlete just wasn't paying attention, or perhaps wasn't concentrating enough. Well, that may be partially true, but I would venture that the way a top athlete's mind works, once they realize that they have a routine play at hand, their brain and body relax just a tiny bit ... and thus, realizing the play in front of them is going to be easy, they automatically start to concentrate on their *next* play.

It's when they do that that the crucial error occurs.

So how do you prevent that from ever happening to you? The easy answer is to simply focus on every play in the game, regardless of how difficult each play is, one at a time. *Do not* look ahead before you finish the immediate task.

Good advice, but of course, that's very hard to maintain during an intense, clutch game. Here's a tip to help you avoid these moments:

Force yourself to stay in the physical moment. That means you can't allow yourself to let your mind wander. *Do not think ahead.* Focus on the present, and let the future action take care of itself.

In a way, this is something of a corollary to "when you think ... you stink." If you allow yourself to start thinking that the routine play is already made—and you're already focusing on the next play—you dramatically increase the odds of muffing the easy play. Of course, that's easier said than done, especially if time is winding down, the crowd is loud and going nuts, and it's a tie score.

But that's when more than ever, you need to focus *in a linear fashion.* Just do one play at a time. Yes, you can be quick about making your layup, but while you're putting the basketball up against the backboard, you need to focus solely on *only* that. Once that is completed, and you see the ball go through the net, *then and only then* should you go to the next play, e.g., hustle back on defense.

You can and should actually practice and visualize these kinds of clutch situations. When most athletes were youngsters, they would go out and fantasize about making the winning shot in the waning moments of a game. You would dribble the ball, imitate a sportscaster's call, and then count down the last seconds on a clock.

Well, do the same thing now that you're older. Be sure to undergo some comparable last-second plays in practice, where you have to make a layup, or make a free throw, or make a tough play on a slow ground ball, or throw a strike during a full count.

But the difference is this: as you go through these last-second game-ending plays, pay full attention to what you're doing. Do not just do it quickly and get it done. Feel and see yourself making each play, and work through each play with a deliberate sense of purpose and accomplishment.

This may all sound like "child's play" and perhaps it is to a certain extent. But in the end, the more you practice these types of last-second routine but important plays, the better and more prepared you're going to feel when confronted by them in a real game. There's nothing more reassuring to know that you have literally practiced, and practiced hard, when it comes to executing these plays. Trust me, you'll never muff or miss an easy play at crunch time ever again.

# 11

# THE GIFT OF ADVERSITY: WHAT IS MENTAL TOUGHNESS?

As I'm sure you know, the term *mental toughness* is commonly used by coaches and scouts all the time. "This kid has shown me some real mental toughness" or "His mental toughness is what drives this young man."

It's one of those terms that is used all the time in sports, but what exactly does it mean?

For me, mental toughness translates into the athlete's inherent ability not only to cope with adversity, but also to have the inner drive and determination to overcome setbacks. You may think that's obvious, but the truth is, having that innate drive, or grit, is not as common as you might think.

Furthermore, I also think it is safe to say that just about every top professional athlete has had to deal with some sort of adversity in their career. I'm sure you know that Michael Jordan, perhaps the greatest basketball player of his generation, was cut from his high school team as a sophomore.

How could that be? How could Michael Jordan not make his high school team in North Carolina? Well, in the coach's opinion, Michael wasn't one of the top players. But here's where mental toughness kicked in. Instead of griping and badmouthing the coach, Jordan went to him and asked what he needed to do in order to improve his game so he could make the varsity squad the next season.

The coach, to his credit, gave him real feedback. Michael listened carefully, and even though he was disappointed about not making the team, he used that adversity to personally drive and motivate himself to become a much improved player. By the time he was a senior in high school, he was on his way to a top career at the University of North Carolina and the NBA.

What's curious is that Jordan's story is not unique. Consider NFL Hall of Famer Steve Young. After having a stellar career in high school in Greenwich, Connecticut, he was recruited to play quarterback at Brigham Young University. But Young was stunned and dismayed when, as he got to his first practice in Provo, Utah, he saw his name was listed as eighth string on the BYU depth chart. He was so low on the depth chart that not only did he not travel for any away games, he didn't dress in uniform for home games either.

Discouraged and upset, Steve called his dad back home in Connecticut, and said he wanted to quit and come home. Steve's dad listened quietly, and finally said, "Steve, you can certainly quit the team, if you want … but you can't come home. I just won't allow that."

That sent a wake-up call to Steve. Adversity was calling. Rather than go home, he decided to devote the rest of that football season and the entire winter to throwing 10,000 spirals in the BYU football facility in order to improve his passing skills. He worked and worked so much that the coaching staff finally began to take notice. It suddenly dawned on them that perhaps they had misjudged Steve's talents as a quarterback. Sure enough, by the time Steve was a senior, he finished runner-up in the Heisman Trophy race, and was named as an All-American quarterback before going on to star with the 49ers.

Again, Steve's ascent to stardom was kick-started because of adversity staring him in the face. To me, those athletes who come to grips with adversity in their careers are those who build a real strength of mental toughness. They know how to bounce back.

## MENTAL TOUGHNESS: DANNY WOODHEAD'S STORY

In the fall of 2016, *The Player's Tribune*, which is Derek Jeter's online platform for top athletes, featured a column by Danny Woodhead, then with the San Diego Chargers and now a member of the Baltimore Ravens. You might recall Danny also played for the Jets and the Patriots. The running back wrote a first-person letter to himself as if he was eighteen years old about all the adversity he was going to face in his football career. It was an interesting perspective. Danny is now in his early thirties, and his reflections were quite moving and powerful.

Keep in mind that Danny has now played in the NFL for close to a decade, so on the surface, he's a big success story. But when he was eighteen and growing up in Nebraska where they grow football players real big, even as a senior in high school, Dan was only 5-foot-7 and 175 pounds. But he did have great speed and fierce determination.

And sure enough, in high school, he became a terrific football player. He even broke the Nebraska state rushing record, pretty impressive for a guy who was relatively small.

Woodhead then waited for the University of Nebraska to contact him. But when they finally did, they basically told him he was just too small to play at the national D-1 level. No scholarship offer.

But Nebraska said he could walk on as a kick returner. But that's about it. No guarantees.

That was the first slap in Danny's face in terms of football adversity.

Not having any other D-1 offers, Woodhead went to Chadron State, a small D-2 school of 3,000 students. He enrolled and he starred as a running back and along the way, he broke the NCAA rushing record. But despite his remarkable college career, he was bypassed by the NFL scouts. Not one team invited him to the scouting combine.

Not surprisingly, Danny went undrafted. But the New York Jets did call him after the draft was over and asked if he would like to sign as an undrafted free agent. Thrilled, he did. But when he got to Jets camp, he tore his ACL. Out for the season.

Then during his second year, having fully recovered from his knee injury, he did well in training camp and made the Jets' final roster. But as the season started, the team decided to let him go.

You get the idea: No Nebraska scholarship. Too small. Not drafted. Gets hurt. Comes back from his injury, makes the final roster, and then gets cut. In short, adversity topped with more adversity.

And yet, as is so often the case with adversity, there's a happy ending in all of this. When Danny and his wife got back to Omaha after being cut by the Jets, he received a call from the New England Patriots. Overjoyed, Danny signed and ended up being a major contributor to to the Patriots' extraordinary legacy of success.

## SO HOW IMPORTANT IS THE ABILITY TO OVERCOME ADVERSITY?

Let's put this rare talent into perspective. In a feature article written by Bill Pennington of the *New York Times* on Theo Epstein, the baseball front office genius who not only transformed the Boston Red Sox franchise into World Series champs, but who also did the same thing with the Chicago Cubs, Epstein was asked what's the most important aspect he asks his baseball scouts about a prospect.

In a word? *Adversity.*

So, for Epstein, someone who grew up and championed analytics in baseball, the key component for a young player is how he handles adversity:

"In the draft room, we will always spend more than half the time talking about the person rather than the player. What are their backgrounds, their psyches, their habits, and what makes them tick.

"And we would ask our scouts to provide three detailed examples of how these young players faced adversity on the field and responded to it, and three examples of how they faced adversity off the field. Because baseball is built on failure. The old expression is that even the best hitter fails seven out of 10 times." (*New York Times*, October 2, 2016.)

In other words, it's pretty clear that for leading baseball mind Theo Epstein, adversity—and knowing how a prospect reacts to when things don't go his way—clearly carries a great deal of weight in determining whether he's worth spending a high draft choice on. Think about that.

## "SUPER ACHIEVERS"—LEATHER vs. ROCK

Ron Wolforth, who is the founder of the well-known Texas Baseball Ranch and is a pitching consultant to many top stars, contends that the premier professional athletes are 1 to 5 percent more resilient than their professional peers. To him, these elite pro athletes have the ability to bounce back from adversity faster than their competitors. In other words, while all of these athletes have faced adversity and setbacks—and while they all have superior physical talent—some of the really elite athletes seem to have an ability to rebound faster and more efficiently.

In the April 22, 2016, issue of *Collegiate Baseball* Wolforth explains: "The best way I can describe this quality form is in detailing the difference between *hard* and *tough*. Many people think that being hard is good. A rock is hard but hit it enough times or with enough force with a hammer and it will eventually start to crack.

"On the other hand, a piece of leather is tough. Hit it all you want with a hammer and it not only doesn't break, you often can't even tell it's been hit at all. The super achievers exhibit higher degrees of leather-like qualities."

Wolforth believes that if you want to continue to climb up the ladder of athletic competition, you need to "practice your ability to return quickly to a deep focus" after being disappointed, distracted, or have to deal with a setback. You need to be totally unshakeable in your core belief that you are leather-tough.

I think that metaphor of leather versus rock is most appropriate for developing athletes. If you can start to visualize that you're taking a leather approach to your athletic career, that's going to serve you well as you play games, deal with difficult coaches, are forced to overcome adversity, and so on. You might even want to set your mind-set and see yourself as a sturdy slab of leather—something that symbolizes that you can take a beating, time and time again, and yet never show any real wear and tear.

My personal sense is that Ron Wolforth is correct that the really preeminent athletes today have this inner, special talent that allows them to be a super-achiever. Names that come to mind would include Tom Brady, Clayton Kershaw, LeBron James, Kevin Durant, Serena Williams, people at that rarified level. Yes, they all have superior physical talent—but so do a lot of other top pro athletes. The difference is that the super achievers have the ability to rise and bounce back quickly from setbacks and are able to propel themselves into being consistent in their performances.

## BOB PETTIT: "THE DRIVE WITHIN ME"

Only serious and longtime basketball fans will remember the NBA career of Bob Pettit. A Hall of Famer, Bob—a 6-foot-9 forward—

was a two-time NBA MVP when he played with the St. Louis Hawks after having starred at LSU. Not too bad for a kid who was cut not once but twice from his high school team in Louisiana.

In his autobiography *The Drive Within Me*, which was written over fifty years ago, Bob wrote about what pushed him to become better at his game. In short, Pettit kept referring to that "inner drive within me" that drove him to work hard at his craft. Whether it was because he had suffered the sting of being cut from his high school team, or for some other reason, the fact remains that Pettit was one of those top athletes who was not going to be outworked by anyone. His Hall of Fame career attests to his success. So what drove Pettit to keep pushing himself?

Again, I'm of the belief (although I cannot prove this) that highly successful athletes are blessed with some sort of almost genetic makeup that propels them to compete and pushes them to outwork their peers as well as their competitors. Even though the human DNA genome has been studied, mapped, and examined in copious detail, I don't believe that they have ever found a genetic component that pinpoints this trait.

That being said, there have been so many examples of extraordinarily talented athletes who also seem to carry a "super" gene for competitiveness. Pettit is one from an earlier time. These are physically gifted individuals who are not only blessed with tremendous and superior physical talent, but their talent is coupled—and amplified—with an internal and tremendous drive to compete and succeed.

No, this key trait can't be taught. It seems to be an internal component that one is born with, like having the unique genetic makeup for blue eyes or big feet. And yet, these superior athletes not only perform well in games, they also work exceedingly hard at their craft in practices as well. They just seem to be driven all the time.

The one aspect I have noticed about these "super" competitive athletes is that they all tend to be most particular and meticulous about their training, their preparation for games, and they are laser-focused on their upcoming opponent. There is rarely any sense that they can relax or take it easy, or that since they have achieved so much along the way, they've now earned a breather. But that's not how they are wired; in fact, it's just the opposite. It's as though they are always ready for their next game, ready for their next opponent.

They seem to carry a sense of true personal responsibility that they are under a certain amount of pressure to perform at a high level in their next contest. That expectation—that pressure—certainly comes from within the athlete. Sure, there is a level of expectation that comes from one's teammates and coach, but ultimately, the real pressure to perform well comes from *inside the individual.*

Again, this is just a personal theory. I have no evidence or research that proves my point. But I guarantee you that if you look around at the truly superior athletes you see in your life, you will find that the ones who win, and win often, are blessed with that innate and superior drive to succeed.

## CAN YOU BECOME LIKE THAT? SHOULD YOU BE LIKE THAT?

When you combine true superior athletic talent with top-notch psychological drive, you are going to have a most formidable foe. Again, of the millions of athletes over the years, only a very small number of athletes have been blessed in this way. These are the athletes who become first-ballot Hall of Famers.

As noted, these kinds of individuals—who have exceptional physical skills and a razor-sharp sense of competition—are hard to find. As for the rest of us, yes, if nothing else, as you encounter these rare athletes as either opponents or as teammates, the best takeaway is for you to recognize just how hard they work at their skills, and how dedicated they are in their practice sessions.

As you begin to appreciate just how good these individuals are, you will find that your own game will start to rise in response. If you want to compete in a serious way with that superstar, you will have to focus that much more on your game in order to be competitive. And that's a good thing. It's as though just being around the hard-working star athletes, you will lift your own game along the way.

That's, of course, a good thing. The superstar athletes' internal drive to succeed has become contagious, and has rubbed off on their teammates.

## "ACT AS IF..."

Let me give you one more approach to step up your game to a higher level. Kathy Delaney-Smith is the winningest college basketball coach in the Ivy League, male or female. She's been the head coach of the Harvard's women's team for more than thirty-five years, and during her tenure, she has won numerous Ivy League champion-ships and has sent a number of her players on to professional careers.

One of her most notable coaching achievements occurred in 1998 when she coached Harvard to a stunning upset over Stanford, 71–67, in the NCAA tournament, the first time a 16-seed defeated a number one seed—and Harvard pulled this upset off at Stanford's home gym.

One of the major tenets of Coach Delaney-Smith is to preach to her players to "act as if"—which means that you need to have the ability to convince yourself that you can indeed raise your game to a higher level, to play with greater intensity, to shoot the ball better, to play better defense, and so on. A strong believer in the power of sports psychology, Coach Delaney-Smith is convinced that one's performance in games is 80 percent mental. Adds Melissa Johnson, one of her former Harvard players: "The body follows where the mind leads."

Indeed, there may be no better explanation of sports psychology than that. Think about that. *Your body will follow where your mind leads you.*

By now, this should all start to sound familiar. Going back to visualization techniques and muscle memory, this is the essence of "training" your mind to think in the right direction and to eliminate distracting emotions, negative thoughts, and self-doubt.

Sure, taking on a difficult opponent is going to present challenges. Yes, you can acknowledge that. But in your preparation—which is something you can and should control—you can plan to take your physical skills to their highest level. And that all starts with your emotional and mental approach.

## WHAT ABOUT ATHLETES WHO HAVE TO COPE WITH REAL GRIEF?

How many times have you tuned in to a big college or pro game, only to hear the commentator say that the star of one of the teams has gone through a major loss in their life away from the field and how in the world is it possible that they are going to be able to perform today when they are undergoing so much emotional distress?

It's a more than valid observation, and obviously, an important storyline to the game.

But most pro coaches know that for highly attuned athletes, while they grieve and mourn just like the rest of us at the sudden loss of a loved one, the athlete looks upon the stadium or arena as a place where they can go to at least distance themselves from the "real world" for a few hours. That's something that isn't often discussed, but the sports pages are filled with such stories.

In *This Is Your Brain on Sports*, the authors Wertheim and Sommers point to numerous such examples of this happening: NFL Hall of Famer Brett Favre heard of the sudden death of his father, who he adored and was very close to, but that didn't stop him from going out and playing a terrific game. Same with Martin St. Louis of the New York Rangers who, during the 2014 playoffs, heard of his mother's sudden passing from a heart attack. But St. Louis played the very next day and in subsequent Stanley Cup games.

The list of these grieving athletes goes on and on, so much so that one could make a case that they might have felt compelled to go forth and play a great game in order to honor their fallen family member. That is, of course, very possible. But my theory is that they went to the playing field and competed within hours of their personal loss as their personal way of coping with grief. In effect, the arena or stadium truly served as their personal sanctuary.

## CONTROLLING ONE'S EMOTIONS IN SPORT

When Jose Fernandez was tragically killed in a boat crash in September 2016, sports fans got a rare glimpse into the emotions of major-league baseball players.

As you recall, the accident happened late on a Saturday night in Miami. The next day, Sunday, the Marlins cancelled their game.

But the next day, Monday, the Marlins did play a game against the New York Mets, who were chasing a postseason playoff bid. The game had to be played.

But in an elegant pregame ceremony, both teams lined up on the third and first baselines as a single trumpeter played "Take Me Out to the Ballgame" in a perfect rendition. When he finished, the hushed ballpark watched something very rare. Members of the opposing teams came together on the infield grass, hugging each other in mutual support, as tears flowed down each player's face.

I recall watching this on television as the players shared their mutual grief for the twenty-four-year-old Fernandez, who was known for his upbeat and outgoing personality. And these athletes showed their human side without any hesitation or embarrassment.

When the television commentators came back on the air as the players eventually made their way back to their respective dugouts, it was the esteemed Ron Darling, the former Mets pitching star now working as a team broadcaster, who captured the essence of this moment. I'm paraphrasing here, but Ron basically reflected that for athletes, they find solace and joy when they go to the ballpark. They leave financial problems, marital concerns, problems with their kids, and so on when they enter the clubhouse and then the dugout. In short, no matter what issues they may have in their own personal world, at the ballpark, the sun is always shining.

I mention all of this, because it was so rare to see so many big-league ballplayers all crying in sorrow. Sports fans almost never see top athletes cry, even when they're in pain from an injury. Indeed, repressing one's emotions in competitive sports has been seen as essential for years. Emotions can only get in the way of your efficiency.

But with the death of Jose Fernandez, the real world got in the way of the sports world.

## 12

# HOW SPORTS PARENTS CAN INTRODUCE THEIR KIDS TO SPORTS PSYCHOLOGY

IN THIS DAY AND AGE where seemingly every sports parent is determined to give their son or daughter every possible advantage or edge they can in athletics, more and more moms and dads are turning to sports psychology in aiding their kids, even when the child is twelve or younger.

For the most part, this is fine. Introducing a youngster to the mental side of competitive sports at a younger age makes sense. There are a few caveats, of course. For starters, you don't want to promise too much to a young athlete. Don't let them assume, for example, that learning how to visualize is a reasonable substitute for real physical practice and more practice. Plus, don't throw too much at them when they're young about how to make adjustments during the heat of a game. And let them get a feel for what it feels like when things aren't going their way in sports. Remember, adversity can be a tremendous motivator.

In my own sports psychology consulting experience, I much prefer to work with top athletes who are either in college or in the pro ranks. That's because I have found that when young athletes run into psychological roadblocks when they are still in middle or even high school, more often than not, the issue is usually rooted not so much in the athlete's performance but with other background issues regarding the relationship between the parent and the athlete.

Of course, this is not always the case, but I have found that many times the real issues blocking a kid's progress have more to do with the psychodynamics of their relationship with their mom and dad than with their actual athletic skills. At that point, it's my sense that the family and the athlete would benefit more from some counseling with a family therapist than with a sports psychology coach.

That being said, I do believe that the right kind of introduction to sports psychology can have some positive aftereffects. The question is, what are the key components, and when should they be introduced?

## AVOID THE POSTGAME ANALYSIS—USE THE PRAISE SANDWICH INSTEAD

I would suggest you start by trying to think back to when you were a youngster and were just finding your way in sports. In order to better understand the pressures that face your kid in sports, try to recall what it was like for you when you were growing up.

For example, start with the basic concept of winning and losing. As adults, we take winning and losing for granted—sometimes you win, sometimes you lose. But kids don't see it that way. To them, and especially when they are very young, they feel that they are *supposed* to win every game. And if they don't, the defeat is viewed as a tremendous unexpected blow to their psyche.

You may have seen a youngster who, devastated by a loss, erupts immediately into tears. As a caring parent, even though you try to console your child, you begin to realize that you will have to explain to them once they have quieted down that if they are going to play sports, then they will have to come to grips with winning *and* losing. This kind of conversation can take place (and it will most likely need to be repeated a few times) when the child turns four or five.

And while it's a wonderful feeling to win, the reality is that they will actually learn more from losing as they progress in sports. Why? Explain to your youngster that while winning is great, the truth is that winning often masks over those parts of their game that really need to be worked on and improved.

But when one loses, those same problem areas in one's skill set begin to become exposed. That's the perfect opportunity for the parent to explain to their child that if they do want to get better, then they will need to learn to focus on those parts of their game that need work.

However, you never do this kind of "postgame analysis" (or PGA as I call it) with your youngster directly after a game, or on the way home from the game in the family SUV. Rather, give your child some time to deal with the pain and with the hurt of the defeat. That's important. Besides, if you try and give them a PGA on the way home, they will not only ignore you, but they will not forgive you for lecturing them on what they did wrong.

Instead, it's better to wait until a quiet moment later in the evening, or even the next day. There's no reason to go over your review and assessment of their game until they are ready for it. And here's another suggestion: give them a "praise sandwich" when you talk about their game.

A praise sandwich does a good job of making sure their fragile and still-developing ego is gently tended to while you give them a subtle but solid piece of constructive criticism.

Let me illustrate: here's an example of a dad talking to his nine-year-old basketball player who handles the ball a lot in a game, but is running the risk of becoming a "ball hog" because he has not learned how to pass the ball off to teammates:

"Joe, I just want you to know how impressed I was with your game today. Your skills at handling the ball are really coming very, very nicely. (This is the first slice of the praise sandwich. By giving a bit of real praise to your son, he will perk up and will be eager to listen to you.)

"And it seems to me that because you see the court so well, if you could somehow learn to pass the ball to some of your other teammates who are open for easy shots, you could really become a major offensive force. (This is the constructive criticism for the boy to learn how to pass the ball more.)

"Because if you can ever master the skill of ball handling and learning how to spot the open man, well, you will become the envy of every basketball coach who is looking for a dynamic point guard."

This entire praise sandwich takes no more than a minute, but if done in a quiet and sincere manner, your youngster will pick up on the advice and will try to make it part of their game starting in the next practice.

Yes, it's that effective.

The overall takeaway is to try and get your young athlete to learn how to dissect their performance in an objective manner—to learn after the game is over what they did well, and more importantly, what they need to do better. That may be the very best lesson you can impart to your youngster. Because in the long run, learning how to self-improve from a careful self-analysis is the pathway to becoming a better athlete.

# HOW TO GET BETTER THROUGH EXPERIMENTATION

Because organized youth sports have become so pervasive everywhere, and it seems that youth coaches are often too focused on winning. That's a concern these days because it's as though kids are no longer allowed any freedom to experiment with their game.

By experiment, I mean that, for example, a kid who is right-handed as a batter tries his luck as a lefty hitter. Or a kid who has just learned how to shoot a basketball changes his approach and tries an entirely different way to see if that new style works better.

Problem is, because youth coaches are so insistent on winning they often chide young athletes from deviating from those skills that they already do well. Too many coaches routinely discourage kids from experimenting with new ways of doing things.

And that, sadly, is not good.

The truth is, kids *do* need to have the freedom to experiment and to try different approaches and styles. Without that freedom, kids run the risk of being locked in too early, and may even become stagnant in their game.

Think of all the unusual batting stances or pitching styles you see at the big-league level. There are literally dozens of different approaches to hitting. No one has ever scientifically proven that one hitting approach is better than another. And with pitchers, some throw with no windup, others pitch from a stretch all the time. Some throw strictly over the top; others are sidewinders.

My point is, all of these big-league pitchers and hitters eventually found a unique approach and style that got them the results they wanted. And to have found that pathway, they had to experiment along the way and take chances on what must have seemed like a radical departure from what their youth coaches or high school coaches taught them. That took some courage, because it's very likely that some youth coach at some point saw them hit or throw differently, and the coach immediately chastised the young player with, "No, don't do it that way ... do it this way ... *this is the right way.*"

You get the idea.

The bottom line is this: As your child learns and masters their sport, if you happen to notice that they want to change their approach, or that they want to tweak their style, don't discourage them. By all means give them the freedom and space to explore for themselves what works, and what doesn't. If they want to try switch-hitting, encourage them. If they want to try a different way of shooting a free throw, let them go for it. If they are working on a trick shot in soccer, that's great.

And remember, there are too many youth coaches these days whose first and immediate reaction is to discourage this kind of experimentation, as though as winning a fifth-grade youth soccer match or Little League baseball game is some sort of big deal. It's not.

Also bear in mind that when kids are allowed the freedom to experiment and to "goof around" in their sport, that also brings forth another key element to the process: a sense of joy and of having fun in one's life. It may sound like a cliché, but sports without a sense of fun will invariably lead to boredom and burnout.

## SHOULD KIDS BE TAUGHT HOW TO VIZUALIZE?

I do not believe it is helpful to introduce the concept of visualization to young athletes (under the age of twelve). Most young athletes lack the necessary requisite experience from playing a lot of sports to know how to capitalize on their previous mistakes and errors in order to train their body and mind on how to correct them.

Talented and gifted athletes under the age of twelve for the most part just rely on their physical skills to compete and to win. There's not a lot of effort or thought put into how they can get better, except perhaps to practice more. I would prefer them to learn the value of watching videotape of themselves in action. That can be a superb teaching tool for young athletes and a lot of fun for them as well. And of course, as they get older, watching and analyzing video of themselves will automatically become a vital part of their development.

And then, once they have seen for themselves how they can improve their game, that's where visualization can be introduced to teach them how to mentally rehearse and correct what they have been doing wrong.

By the way, when young athletes do start to watch video of their performances, you can help them start learning how to maximize the experience by advising them to first just watch the video a few times to enjoy themselves. Let them bask in the fun of the video. Let them have that joyful experience a few times without even giving a second thought to what they did right or what they did wrong.

But then, after the thrill has subsided a bit, you can then sit with them in a more serious moment, and go through key plays with them. Ask them, in a quiet and gentle way, about what they learned from what they did well during these critical plays. And more importantly, when the video reveals poor plays or mistakes in judgment, ask them what they could take away from that, and how could they learn to improve. Be careful not to be too harsh in your manner. Again, you want this to be fun for your child, not a painful lesson.

## HOW TO AVOID BURNOUT

The very best way to avoid having your child become tired or bored with their sport is to make sure that they get "built-in" weeks away from games and practice. By doing that, you ensure that if they go on vacation from their sport for a week several times during the year that they will almost long to get back into the competition again.

On the other hand, if they don't get some time off, they will sometimes begin to see their "play" as "work" and they will lose their interest and their drive. When that transition occurs, your child is beginning to run the risk of burnout.

Most kids tend to burn out between the ages of eleven and thirteen. Many of them do so because they have specialized in just one sport over the last few years, and as their involvement and focus becomes pretty much year round, their initial passion for that sport often gradually wears down. Remember, kids can get bored easily.

To prevent this from happening, take a proactive approach. As noted, make sure that at the end of each season your child gets at least a week off from all games and practice. Don't take no for an answer. Better yet, see if you can plan a family vacation for a week so that your youngster is involved in other fun activities that have nothing at all to do with their sport.

Another solid approach, which is especially helpful for kids who have specialized in one sport, is to get them to play other sports. It doesn't have to be the same kind of full-on commitment that they make to their primary sport. But if they are good athletes, chances are they will enjoy playing on other school or intramural teams. That kind of diversion is not only a good way to keep them from burning out on their main sport, but they'll discover new friends, new talents, and new ways in which to enjoy sports and competition.

And then, when they do return to their main sport, they'll come back refreshed and reinvigorated, which is the perfect tonic to avoiding any kind of burnout.

According to most recent studies, today's athletic kids are specializing in one sport more than ever, and at earlier ages. Unfortunately, there's not much we can do to prevent that trend. However, it's up to the parent to be on the lookout for potential signs of burnout with their athlete, as that has become a problem which is also more epidemic than ever. You may not hear about it much, but sadly, more and more kids are walking away from the highly pressurized world of competitive athletics when they are still in middle or high school. And once they walk away, they rarely come back.

A generation or two ago, terms like burnout really didn't exist. That's because most young athletes rarely specialized in just one sport growing up. They played different sports according to the changing seasons, e.g., football or soccer in the fall, basketball or ice hockey in the winter, and baseball, lacrosse, or tennis in the spring.

In fact, it was the rare athlete who played only one sport the entire year. True, in some individual sports, such as swimming or gymnastics, kids did tend to spend a good portion of their youth focusing on just one sport. And indeed, I think it's fair to say that some of those young swimmers or gymnasts became the first victims of burnout. To spend copious amounts of time in the pool each day or on the balance beam in order to improve and hone their skills often led to a questioning or a concern that perhaps they were missing out on other aspects of growing up.

In my experience, burnout tends to develop when an athlete reaches a point where they consciously begin to ask questions about whether they are missing out on other things in life, such as hanging out with friends, going to parties, sleepovers, etc. Or, they see how much enjoyment their school friends have in being involved in a variety of sports and activities.

Problem is, when you're eight or ten years old, and you show a talent for an individual sport which demands a year-round commitment, most kids dutifully follow what their parents ask of them. No questions asked. But when the youngster gets to be twelve or thirteen, and they become more aware of their surroundings and peers, it's at that point when they begin to starting asking questions about their total devotion to this one sport.

And when kids start pushing back, e.g., "Can't I miss practice today?" or, "Why can't I go to my friend's sleepover party?" it's at that point that they begin to start wondering whether this solitary devotion to one sport is the answer. Burnout is not often far behind.

In order to avoid these potential burnout issues as your child reaches middle school age, keep in mind the built-in break approach. And there's certainly nothing wrong with allowing your child to have a sleepover or to go to a birthday party or to do a number of the other kinds of fundamental activities that all kids their age are enjoying.

When you say to your child, "I'm sorry, but you can't go to your friend's party" simply because your child has an early practice the next day, as a parent, you may want to rethink your priorities for your youngster.

In other words, in the long run, it's certainly OK for your child to miss a practice or two along the way.

## GRANT HILL: "PACKING TWO PARACHUTES IN LIFE"

One of the most important and vital life lessons you need to impart to your kid is the concept of packing two parachutes in life.

This is a concept that I first learned about from former Duke and NBA star Grant Hill. Even though it was apparent early on that Grant was a gifted soccer and basketball player while growing up in suburban Virginia, his parents, Calvin and Janet Hill, knew how quickly a promising career in sports could disappear due to an injury or other unexpected developments. Perhaps it was because Calvin himself had been an All-Pro running back with the Dallas Cowboys after graduating from Yale, he knew firsthand how quickly the best laid plans for athletic stardom go away. Regardless, Grant's parents made sure that he understood how precarious a career in sports is.

As a result, and I'm paraphrasing here, they always cautioned him to pack two parachutes in life, meaning that if his first dream, or parachute, didn't open, then at least he had the foresight to have packed a second one, just in case. This is very smart advice, and for any sports parent who want to make sure that their youngster is prepared for the unexpected ups and downs of life, this is an essential lesson.

It makes no difference what that second parachute, or dream, is. Your child may have a passion for computer programming, or for teaching, or for wanting to become a doctor. It doesn't really make any difference what the other passion is—all that matters is that they develop the same kind of love for that other "parachute" in life as they have for sports.

The point is, when their transition from the sports world is finally upon them—and trust me, this transition happens to every top athlete—the move to a new pursuit is a lot easier if they already have a good idea of what they're eager to do next in life. That's, of course, the second parachute.

Too many athletes spend so much of their time focusing on just one dream—that of being an athlete—that they miss out on life's other possibilities. Then, when they retire or are released, they often find themselves floundering, trying to figure out what their next career might be. It can be a very difficult and trying process for them.

From a parental perspective, it makes no difference if they are superstars or are destined to be nothing more than high school players. Teach them to find a secondary passion in life. That's your job as a sports parent.

# ONE MORE NOTE—THE JOY OF PLAYING AT THE ELITE LEVEL

CATEGORIZE THIS STORY UNDER "SOMETIMES you have to take a break and smell the roses."

One sunny afternoon a few years ago, I was making the rounds in the outfield in Cleveland where most of the pitchers were shagging flies during batting practice. I found myself chatting with Tom Candiotti, the outstanding knuckleball pitcher. Candy, who was always in good spirits, was in an especially good mood that afternoon.

So I asked him why.

He gave me a big smile, and then looked around the outfield to make sure the other pitchers couldn't overhear him, and then quietly said to me: "Rick, I just signed a huge, multimillion-dollar contract with the Indians."

I was, of course, thrilled for Candy, and congratulated him. He certainly deserved the big payday. Here's a guy who had made his way into professional baseball as an undrafted player, and had worked his tail off to advance from one level of the minors to the next. There was no glamor in any of this. Just hard work, a strong and firm belief in his knuckleball, and a desire to see whether this unusual pitch would take him anywhere in the game. And sure enough, Candy made it to the bigs, where he enjoyed a long and very prosperous career.

But here's the best part.

After Tom had told me about the contract being signed, he then looked around the outfield again, and said to me in an almost conspiratorial tone: "Rick, they're going to pay me *millions* to pitch in the big leagues ... this is my dream come true."

And then he paused, reflected, and added:

"The truth is ... I would have paid *them* to allow me to pitch here."

# SUMMARY OF KEY POINTS

WE HAVE COVERED A LOT of ground in this book in an attempt to cut through all the clutter of the psychology of sports. To that end, here are the key components that any serious athlete should learn and master in terms of their own unique mental preparation to competitive sports:

Make visualization into an active part of your day

Build your muscle memory

Let your mind lead your body

Design both your pregame as well as your postgame mental routine

Transform yourself into leather, not rock

Write and constantly refer to your mental cue card

Find your unique focal point, if needed

# SELECTED BIBLIOGRAPHY

## BOOKS

Ankiel, Rick. *The Phenomenon: Pressure, the Yips, and the Pitch that Changed My Life*, Free Press, 2017.

Beilock, Sian. *Choke: What the Secrets of the Brain Reveal About Getting It Right When You Have To*, Atria, 2011.

Canfield, Jack and Mark Victor Hansen. "18 Holes in His Mind" in *A 2nd Helping of Chicken Soup for the Soul*, Health Communications, 1995.

Colvin, Geoff. *Talent Is Overrated: What Really Separates World-Class Performers from Everybody Else*, Portfolio, 2008.

Coop, Richard H. *Mind over Golf: How to Use Your Head to Lower Your Score*, John Wiley & Sons, 1997.

Csikszentmihalyi, Mihaly. *Flow: The Psychology of Optimal Experience*, HarperCollins, 2008.

Dorfman, H. A. *The Mental ABC's of Pitching: A Handbook for Performance Enhancement*, Diamond Communications, 2001.

_____. *The Mental Game of Baseball: A Guide to Peak Performance*, Diamond Communications, 2002.

_____. *The Mental Keys to Hitting: A Handbook of Strategies for Performance Enhancement*, Diamond Communications, 2001.

_____. *Coaching the Mental Game: Leadership Philosophies and Strategies for Peak Performance in Sports—and Everyday Life*, Taylor Publishing, 2005.

Duckworth, Angela. *Grit: The Power of Passion and Perseverance*, Scribner, 2016.

Epstein, David. *The Sports Gene: Inside the Science of Extraordinary Athletic Performance*, Current, 2013.

Ericsson, Anders and Robert Pool. *Peak: Secrets from the New Science of Expertise*, Houghton Mifflin Harcourt, 2016.

Fader, Jonathan. *Life as Sport: What Top Athletes Can Teach You about How to Win in Life*, Da Capo Press, 2016.

Gallwey, W. Timothy. *The Inner Game of Tennis*, Random House, 1974.

Hanson, Tom. *Play Big:* Mental Toughness Secrets That Take Baseball Players to the Next Level, Hanson House, 2011.

Loehr, James E. *The New Toughness for Training for Sports: Mental, Emotional, and Physical Conditioning from One of the World's Premier Sports Psychologists*, Plume, 1995.

Maltz, Maxwell, M.D. *Psycho-Cybernetics: A New Way to Get More Living Out of Life*, Prentice-Hall, 1960.

Maher, Charlie. *The Complete Mental Game of Baseball: Taking Charge of the Process, on and Off the Field*, Author House, 2011.

McGinn, Daniel. *Psyched Up: How the Science of Mental Preparation Can Help You Succeed*, Portfolio, 2017.

Moyer, Jamie and Larry Platt. *Just Tell Me I Can't: How Jamie Moyer Defied the Radar Gun and Defeated Time*, Grand Central, 2013.

Orlick, Terry. *In Pursuit of Excellence*, Human Kinetics, 1980.

Peterson, Rick, and Judd Hoekstra. *Crunch Time: How to Be Your Best When it Matters Most*, Berrett-Koehler Publishers, 2017.

Ravizza, Ken, and Tom Hanson. *Heads-Up Baseball: Playing the Game One Pitch at a Time*, McGraw-Hill, 1998.

Rotella, Bob. *How Champions Think: In Sports and in Life*, Simon & Schuster, 2015.

_____. *Golf Is Not a Game of Perfect*, Simon & Schuster, 1995.

Sullivan, Paul. *Clutch: Excel Under Pressure*, Portfolio, 2012.

Wertheim, L. Jon, and Sam Sommers. *This Is Your Brain on Sports: The Science of Underdogs, the Value of Rivalry, and What We Can Learn from the T-Shirt Cannon*, Crown Archetype, 2016.

Weisinger, Hendrie, and J. P. Pawliw-Fry. *Performing Under Pressure: The Science of Doing Your Best When it Matters Most*, Crown Business, 2015.

## PERIODICALS

Bialik, Carl, "The Power of Lucky Charms," *Wall Street Journal*, April 29, 2010.

Cain, Brian, "Value of the Mental Game," *Collegiate Baseball*, May 6, 2016.

Carson, Howie J. and Dave Collins, "Implementing the Five-A Model of Technical Refinement: Key Roles of the Sports Psychologist, *Journal of Applied Sport Psychology*, 28, 392–409, 2016.

Chen, Albert, "The Pitch Doctor," *Sports Illustrated*, March 28, 2016.

_____, "Yippee Ki-yazy," *Sports Illustrated*, August 31, 2015.

Crouse, Karen, "Andrew Toles Goes from Frozen Foods to Dodgers' Outfield," *New York Times*, October 20, 2016.

Ferguson, Doug, "Willett Wins the Masters," Associated Press, April 11, 2016.

Goode, Erica, "To Yankee Second Baseman, Throwing Is No Idle Thought," *New York Times*, June 17, 2000.

Meyers, Naila-Jean, "U.S. Open Today: Andy Murray Falls: Serena Williams Survives," *New York Times*, September 7, 2016.

Pavlovich, Lou Jr., "Power of Mind Exploited at Arizona," *Collegiate Baseball*, October 1, 2016.

_____, "Can Optimal Experiences Become Norm in Game?" *Collegiate Baseball*, February 12, 2015.

_____, "Control How You Respond to Situations," *Collegiate Baseball*, April 22, 2016.

Pennington, Bill, "A Team's Cursed Century Warrants a Proven Savior," *New York Times*, October 2, 2016.

_____, "To Calm His Jittery Nerves, Keegan Bradley Embraces Them," *New York Times*, July 15, 2016.

Schonbrun, Zach, "Honing the Gymnastics of the Brain," *New York Times*, January 8, 2017.

Simonsmeier, Bianca A. and Susanne Buecker, "Interrelations of Imagery Use, Imagery Ability, and Performance in Young Athletes, and Performance in Young Athletes, *Journal of Applied Sport Psychology*, 29, 32–43, 2017.

Smith, Rory, "To Put Ball in the Net, Dutch Clubs Shoot Space Aliens First," *New York Times*, March 5, 2017.

# ACKNOWLEDGMENTS

I KNOW FIRSTHAND HOW DIFFICULT and time consuming it is to manage a book from its original idea stage all the way to a finished product. I also know that in order to launch a book successfully, it's always truly a team effort in every way.

To that end, I first and foremost want to thank my longtime friend and associate Ken Samelson for his superb guidance, endless patience, and much-needed assistance in seeing this project through. I had the distinct privilege of working with Ken for years on *The Baseball Encyclopedia*, and his attention to detail and precise record-keeping was truly remarkable in every way. And the editorial skills he exhibited on that book have carried over in this book.

But when it comes to book publishing, just writing and editing a book is half the job. To that end, I want to salute and thank Bill Wolfsthal for doing such a wonderful job in directing and overseeing the sales of the book into the right outlets. I also want to single out Marion Schwaner for doing such a great job in publicizing and promoting the book, and Sarah Jones for always being there for me during the production process.

And of course, I want to thank my beautiful wife, Trish, and the rest of my family for being so patient with me as I wrote this book over the last few years. This work represents a lifetime of my education in the world of sports psychology, all the way from my undergraduate years in college and in graduate school in the 1970s and 1980s through my mentoring from Harvey Dorfman and continuing all the way to the present day.

# INDEX

## ALSO BY THE AUTHOR

THE PSYCHOLOGY OF WINNING BASEBALL

HARVARD BOYS

WHAT'S A NICE HARVARD BOY LIKE YOU DOING IN THE BUSHES?

COACHING KIDS FOR DUMMIES

# ABOUT THE AUTHOR

RICK WOLFF IS A NATIONALLY recognized expert in the field of sports psychology. Often interviewed by the national media about the mental pressures that confront today's athletes, Wolff has written and lectured widely on the psychological issues that are intertwined with top athletic performance.

Wolff, a former professional baseball player in the Detroit Tigers organization, also served as the roving sports psychology coach for the Cleveland Indians from 1989 to 1994. Over the years, he's worked with numerous top professional and collegiate athletes, including players from the NFL, NBA, NHL, and MLB. He's a direct protégé of the famed sports psychology coach Harvey Dorfman.

Wolff also served as the head baseball coach at Mercy College from 1978 to 1985 when the Flyers were nationally ranked in the NCAA (Div. II). He was inducted into the Mercy College Athletics Hall of Fame in 2008.

He graduated magna cum laude in psychology from Harvard University where he played varsity baseball, and received his Master's degree with high honors in psychology from Long Island University. Wolff is heard every Sunday morning on WFAN Sports Radio in New York City on his highly popular *The Sports Edge* show where he discusses key and timely issues in sports psychology and in sports parenting. For a decade he wrote hundreds of columns for *Sports Illustrated* on the issues centering on youth and amateur sports. Over the years he's been interviewed on sports psychology and sports parenting issues on every major television and cable network and sports outlet; he even did an entire show with Oprah Winfrey.

Much in demand as a public speaker and seminar leader, Wolff also continues to work with select top athletes on their mental approach to   sports. He can be reached at www.askcoachwolff.com, or via email at askcoachwolff@gmail.com.

Wolff lives in Armonk, NY, with his wife Trish. They have three grown children: John, Alyssa, and Samantha.